SANCHO

MATT AND TOM OLDFIELD

ULTIMATE FOOTBALL HEROES

SANCHO

FROM THE PLAYGROUND
TO THE PITCH

DINO

First published by Dino Books in 2022,
an imprint of Bonnier Books UK,
4th Floor, Victoria House, Bloomsbury Square, London WC1B 4DA
Owned by Bonnier Books,
Sveavägen 56, Stockholm, Sweden

@UFHbooks
@footieheroesbks
www.heroesfootball.com
www.bonnierbooks.co.uk

Text © Matt Oldfield 2022
The right of Matt Oldfield to be identified as the author of this work has been
asserted by him in accordance with the Copyright, Designs and Patents Act 1988.

Design by www.envydesign.co.uk

Paperback ISBN: 978 1 78946 478 8
E-book ISBN: 978 1 78946 479 5

British Library cataloguing-in-publication data:
A catalogue record for this book is available from the British Library.

Printed and bound in Great Britain by Clays Ltd, Elcograf S.p.A.

1 3 5 7 9 10 8 6 4 2

For all readers,
young and old(er)

Matt Oldfield is an accomplished writer and the editor-in-chief
of football review site Of Pitch & Page. Tom Oldfield is a
freelance sports writer and the author of biographies on
Cristiano Ronaldo, Arsène Wenger and Rafael Nadal.

Cover illustration by Dan Leydon.
To learn more about Dan visit danleydon.com
To purchase his artwork visit etsy.com/shop/footynews
Or just follow him on Twitter @danleydon

TABLE OF CONTENTS

ACKNOWLEDGEMENTS

First of all, I'd like to thank everyone at Bonnier Books UK for supporting me throughout and for running the ever-expanding UFH ship so smoothly. Writing stories for the next generation of football fans is both an honour and a pleasure. Thanks also to my agent, Nick Walters, for helping to keep my dream job going, year after year. A special thanks also goes to Ryan Baldi for being so generous with his time, talent and knowledge of all things Sancho.

Next up, an extra big cheer for all the teachers, booksellers and librarians who have championed these books, and, of course, for the readers. The success of this series is truly down to you.

Okay, onto friends and family. I wouldn't be writing this series if it wasn't for my brother Tom. I owe him so much and I'm very grateful for his belief in me as an author. I'm also very grateful to the rest of my family, especially Mel, Noah, Nico, and of course Mum and Dad. To my parents, I owe my biggest passions: football and books. They're a real inspiration for everything I do.

Pang, Will, Mills, Doug, Naomi, John, Charlie, Sam, Katy, Ben, Karen, Ana (and anyone else I forgot) – thanks for all the love and laughs, but sorry, no I won't be getting 'a real job' anytime soon!

And finally, I couldn't have done any of this without Iona's encouragement and understanding. Much love to you.

CHAPTER 1

ENGLAND'S NEW WING WIZARD

10 September 2019, St Mary's Stadium, Southampton

'You ready, J?' Raheem Sterling asked as the England players waited in the tunnel before kick-off against Kosovo. It was an important Euro 2020 qualifier and Jadon was making only his fourth senior start, in place of Manchester United's Marcus Rashford, but he was still all smiles and no nerves, as always.

'Of course – I'm always ready, bro!' Jadon replied. The pressure didn't bother him because although he was still only nineteen years old, he had already played over fifty first-team games for his German club, Borussia Dortmund. Now, it was time to star for his country too. 'Tonight's the night – I'm going to score my first England goal and you're going to set me up, Raz, just like I set you up against Croatia, remember? Pleeeeaaaase!'

Jadon already had two international assists, but he was desperate to grab his first goal for England.

'We'll see about that!' Raheem laughed. He knew Jadon well from his early days at the Manchester City academy, and he reminded him so much of himself when he was younger – skilful, fearless and full of confidence. It didn't really matter whether he was in the park with his mates, or wearing a white England shirt in front of thousands of fans – Jadon just loved playing football and entertaining people with his tricks.

So, what could he do tonight to make the crowd at St Mary's go 'Woah!'? With Raheem on the left and Jadon on the right, England had two of the most exciting wingers in world football, and in the middle, they had Harry Kane, one of the sharpest shooters in the game. What a fantastic front three – surely the goals were going to flow!

The first goal arrived after only thirty seconds, but it was Kosovo who scored it, not England. Uh-oh! It was a real shock, but the England players didn't panic – there was plenty of time left to turn things around. In fact, it didn't take them long at all. Seven minutes later, Raheem headed in an equaliser, and soon, England were 3–1 up, thanks to a strike from Harry Kane and then an own goal from Mërgim Vojvoda.

Jadon was the one who had created the own goal by weaving his way into the box at speed before sending a dangerous cross into the six-yard box. It was meant for Raheem, but the ball bounced off a Kosovo defender instead and into the net.

'Nice one, J!' Harry shouted, giving his fellow attacker a double high-five. Jadon was pleased with his performance so far, but now he was desperate to grab a goal of his own...

With half-time approaching, Raheem raced up the left wing to launch another England counter-attack. As he looked up, he spotted Jadon in the space on the right side of the box, calling for it. Raheem thought about shooting himself, but he knew that if he didn't

set his friend up, he would be hearing about it for
days.

PING!

When the pass arrived, Jadon didn't rush. He had
to get this right – it was a golden chance he couldn't
waste, so first, he took a touch to control the ball and
steady himself. Even as a defender dived in for a last-
ditch block, Jadon kept his cool. He just shifted the
ball a little to the right and then with a swing of his
leg, he fired a low shot past the keeper. *4–1!*

*Goooooooooooooooooooooaaaaaaaaaaaaaaaaallllllllllllll
lllllllllllll!!!!!!!!!!!!!!!!!!!!*

His first for England – what a proud moment! As he
jogged over to the corner flag, Jadon punched the air
and kissed the Three Lions on the badge of his shirt.
Then, as a big grin spread across his face, he turned
around and pointed at a very important teammate:

'Cheers, Raz!'

For Jadon, it was a childhood dream come true to
score for his country, especially with all his family
watching, and he wasn't done yet. Two minutes later,
Raheem dribbled forward again and set up Jadon for

his second goal of the game.

'Yesssssss – thanks bro, you're the best!'

England's wing wizards were on fire – 5–1! First Raheem and now, Jadon, the new wonderkid on the scene. Although he couldn't quite complete his hat-trick, he carried on terrorising the Kosovo defenders with his dazzlingly quick feet, much to the delight of the supporters in the stadium.

Woah!... Yeah!... Wow!

They had all heard about the exciting young winger who was doing so well at Dortmund, and now they had seen him at his electric best for England.

After eighty-five minutes of attacking magic, Jadon's job was done. As the fans cheered him off the field, he clapped and clapped and clapped. It was an emotional night that he would never, ever forget.

When Jadon reached the touchline, Gareth Southgate was waiting for him with a big smile and a pat on the back. Before the match, the England manager had challenged him to take his opportunity, and boy, had Jadon succeeded! With two goals and an assist, he had proved that he was ready to represent his country at the highest level.

Jadon's rapid and remarkable rise to the top continued. At the age of nineteen, the street footballer from South London was now all set to become an England superstar.

CHAPTER 2

A FOOTBALL-CRAZY KID IN KENNINGTON

Once the school day was over and all the kids had dropped their bags at home, that's when playtime really began.

'Come on, let's go!' Jadon called out impatiently, his words echoing around the estate. The Guinness Trust Buildings in Kennington were made up of two main blocks of flats, with a concrete space in the middle. That's where Jadon stood, with a football at his feet as always, and while he waited for his friends to join him, he worked on his keepy-uppies:

...15 ...16... 17...18...

Not bad at all, especially for a six-year-old! If he kept practising, Jadon was sure that he'd be able to do fifty soon. The concrete courtyard was fine for doing a few keepy-uppies, but he preferred to show off his full range of football skills, and for that, it was much better to play on the caged pitch behind the estate. 'Blue Park' was what everyone called it because that was the colour of the poles of the basketball hoops that stood tall at either end. The pitch was mostly used for football matches, though, and it often got busy. Plus, it would get dark soon, and he would become impatient if his friends were slow to turn up.

'HURRY UP!'

'COMING, J!'

One by one, young kids rushed out of their flats to join Jadon in the middle. As well as being the best player on the estate for his age, he also had a ball, and together, those two things made him the obvious ringleader.

'Right, ready?' his friend Ryan suggested eventually, jumping up and down to keep himself warm.

Nearly, but Jadon had one quick thing he wanted to do before they went. He couldn't help it. 'Wait, try to tackle me first.'

Really? Although Ryan was a good defender, he didn't fancy his chances. He tried his best to keep his eyes on the ball and not the blur of Jadon's dancing feet, but everything was moving so fast. Eventually, Ryan lunged towards the ball, but instead of winning it, he watched it roll through his own legs.

'MEGS!' Jadon shouted joyfully as he collected the ball on the other side. 'AGAIN!'

'Woaahhh, how did you do that?' his friend Mo marvelled.

'Magic,' Jadon replied with a cheeky smile and a shrug. 'Right, everyone ready? Let's go!'

When they arrived at Blue Park, a group of bigger kids from the estate were already playing a proper game, but they managed to find just enough room for their own mini-match. Not that Jadon needed much room; he loved a challenge and he could squeeze his way out of any space, the smaller the better.

'Go on, get it off me if you can!'

Flicks, tricks, stepovers and body swerves – Jadon could do them all already, and that's why he was so amazing at one-v-ones. Which way would he go?

What skill would he show off next? Most of the time, it was impossible to stop him. Nothing made him happier than having a ball at his feet and a defender to beat. School was okay, but football was definitely his favourite thing in the whole world, and he would have played all day and all night if he was allowed.

'We want you home by 5.30,' his parents had told him again and again, 'and not a minute later! You understand?'

'Yes Mum, yes Dad!'

Jadon knew that they worried about him getting into trouble on the streets of South London, but he wasn't interested in any of the bad, dangerous things that some of the bigger kids around him were doing. No – he just wanted to play football!

When Jadon was dribbling with the ball, it was like nothing else mattered. He could escape from the darker side of life on the estate, and also from his own personal sadness. It was now a year since his baby brother had tragically died, but he still thought about him all the time. He had even written a poem at primary school about all of the things they would have done together:

'I couldn't wait till you grew up,

teach you football and win the cup.'

Sadly, Jadon would never get the chance to share his skills with him, but the pain made him even more determined to achieve his dream of becoming a top professional footballer. His brother was his main inspiration and playing for Chelsea or Manchester United – and maybe even England too! – would be the perfect way to do him proud.

'One day, baby boy. One day, I'm gonna be a superstar...'

Sometimes, when he got tired of making his friends look like fools, Jadon stopped to watch the bigger kids play. Their massive, end-to-end matches were really entertaining, with everyone competing to see who could pull off the sickest skills and score the greatest goals. For Jadon as a spectator, it looked like so much fun, plus it was a great way to learn about lots of cool new tricks.

'Woah! Guys, did you see that one? Unreal!'

Eyes wide with excitement, Jadon tried to

memorise every move, so that he could go away and practise them, preparing for the important day when he would be allowed to join in too.

CHAPTER 3

TAKING ON THE BIG KIDS AT BLUE PARK

Football – if you're good enough, then you're old enough to play. After only a few days in Reception at Crampton Primary School, tiny but talented Jadon had been asked if he wanted to join in with the Year 5s and 6s, and it was a similar story at Blue Park. Without him realising it, the bigger kids had been watching the way he made his friends look like fools, and soon they thought he was ready to step up and play football with them.

Really? Already? Wow, cool – what a compliment! With a cheeky smile and his usual confidence, Jadon said yes straight away. He couldn't wait to show the bigger kids what he could do with the ball. This was an amazing opportunity to put his one-v-one tekkers to the test in a proper game against proper players.

Before he could shine, however, Jadon had lots to learn about street football:

1) Teams played without tactics, positions, or any organisation. Basically, it was just a fun free-for-all with your friends, and with so many people running around a really small space, the pace of the game was frantic! When you got the ball, you had to think fast and move fast – really, really fast. 'Use it or lose it', as people liked to say.

Hey, next time, pass the ball quicker!

2) Although everyone knew each other from the estate, the games were very competitive and often very aggressive too. The ball wasn't the only thing that bounced off the walls of the cage; the bodies of players did too as they barged each other and battled for possession. Barely a day went by without an angry argument and some pushing and shoving. Jadon was the newest, youngest and shortest player on the pitch, but that didn't mean the bigger kids were going to go easy on him. Oh no, everyone was treated equally!

Watch out, you're playing with the big boys now!

3) If Jadon fell over on the concrete and hurt himself, that didn't always mean it was a foul and it definitely didn't always mean it was a free kick.

Nah, toughen up, kid – I barely touched you!

The rules were more relaxed in street football, and there weren't any referees, so there wasn't much point in complaining. It was best to just get back up and carry on playing.

'Come on, I can do this!'

In such a challenging environment, a lot of young footballers lost confidence when their tricks didn't work and they kept losing the ball – but not Jadon. No, even as a small six-year-old, nothing seemed to faze him. He really enjoyed the style, the energy and the creativity of street football, and so if at first he didn't succeed, he just tried and tried again until eventually he did.

As he dribbled the ball forward in a blur of dancing feet, Jadon swerved his body to the left and then to the right. Which trick was he going to try and which way would he go? The defender in front of him couldn't work it out, but he had to make a decision, and fast. In the end, he went to his left, which turned out to be a big mistake. Because as soon as he lunged in for the tackle, Jadon slid the ball straight through his legs like it was the simplest skill in the world.

'MEGS!'

4) In street football, no-one really cared about goals because there were always lots of those; the thing that mattered most was skills. When your trick finally worked and everyone went 'Woah!', that was the best feeling in the world and all your earlier mistakes were forgotten.

'Nice one, J – that was SICK!'

Jadon's face beamed as brightly as the floodlights above them. Yessssss, he was shining at last!

Thanks to that early football education on the caged pitches of Kennington, Jadon's ball control got better and better, and so did his dribbling and his decision-making. The kids he was playing against were bigger and stronger than him, but he knew that if he attacked with the right speed and skills, he could still get past them. That was the challenge, and the more he practised, the more unstoppable he became at Blue Park. Soon, it was time for Jadon to take the next step in his superstar journey: joining a top football club.

CHAPTER 4

WATFORD'S NEW WONDERKID!

At the young age of seven, Jadon had his first big football decision to make: Arsenal or Watford? Scouts from both academies had spotted his talent, but which club should he choose?

In terms of first-team talent, the answer was obvious: Arsenal all the way! The Gunners had just finished in the Premier League Top Four, and they had superstars like Cesc Fàbregas, Robin van Persie and Thierry Henry in their squad. Watford, meanwhile, had been relegated back down to the league below, the Championship.

For Jadon and his family, however, there were other things to think about too. Most importantly, location, because how was he going to get to training three nights a week? Jadon's parents wouldn't always be able to take him because they both worked really hard, so sometimes he would have to take public transport on his own instead.

The Watford academy turned out to be a slightly easier place to get to from South London, and so in the end, that's where Jadon went. It was still a two-hour journey away from his home, but it was worth it to play the game he loved at a higher level.

At first, arriving at Watford felt like entering a totally different world of football. From the concrete cages of Kennington, suddenly Jadon was now playing on a soft carpet of perfectly cut grass with white sidelines instead of walls. And away from the frantic chaos of street football, suddenly he was now playing a much calmer version of the game with proper organisation and positions. Arggh, where was he supposed to go and what was he supposed to do? It was like a totally different sport!

'He's clearly very good, but he's going to need to adapt' – that's what Dave Godley, the Watford youth coach, thought when he first watched Jadon at training. In terms of pure technique and skill, the small boy was sensational, a long way ahead of a lot of his new teammates. The problem, however, was that Jadon had no experience of playing club football.

Defending?

Marking?

Winger vs central striker?

No – all Jadon really knew and loved was getting the ball and attacking, by gliding and tricking his way past as many players as possible. That was fine if it worked, but football was a game that involved more than just individual skill. Still, if the Watford youth coaches could teach Jadon the street footballer about teamwork and tactics, he certainly had the potential to become a very special player indeed.

'If there's no way through, lift your head up and look for a teammate to pass to instead.'

'You don't need to show off all your skills every time you get the ball. Sometimes, it's best to keep things simple.'

'Don't drop so deep – you're our striker today, so

we need you to stay up front.'

Within weeks, Jadon was already starting to shine at Watford. As he'd shown before with the bigger kids at Blue Park, he was a fast and determined learner, and he had the confidence to keep trying and trying until he succeeded. While he refused to say goodbye to his street football flair completely, he was happy to add new skills to his game, especially if they helped him to stand out and become the best young player at the football club. That was the goal, however hard he had to work to get there.

'Well done, Jadon – what a pass that was!'

'Yes, J – that's exactly what I was talking about!'

'That's it – use your speed to run behind the defence and score!'

Although Godley was really pleased with Jadon's rapid progress, it gave him a different problem to worry about. Young players were allowed to sign a contract with a club at the age of eight, but Jadon was still only seven and he was already attracting a lot of attention from other teams in the area. One was Chelsea; the Premier League giants were on a mission to sign up all of South London's finest young footballers.

Uh-oh! Nooooo, were Watford about to lose yet another talented academy player? No, not this time; Godley made sure of it. When Jadon's eighth birthday finally arrived, the youth coach waited at the train station to pick the boy and his family up and drive them to the training ground himself. That way, no big bad club could snatch him away!

Jadon sat down to sign his first contract with a big smile on his face. He was on his way, one step closer to his professional football dream. Move over Ashley Young and Marvin Sordell – Watford had a new wonderkid!

CHAPTER 5

JADON AND REISS: YOUNG STARS OF SOUTH LONDON

Although Jadon was now all set to become Watford's new wonderkid, that didn't stop him from starring for other teams too. He was still the same old football-crazy kid from Kennington, with a ball always at his feet, and he loved the game far too much to stay at home and rest. Whenever he had a free moment, he headed back out onto the local caged pitches to practise his skills and carry on making his friends look like fools.

'MEGS!'

Watford were based north of the River Thames, but Jadon would forever be a proud South Londoner. So, when he was asked if he wanted to play for

Southwark in the Under-11s football competition at the 2011 London Youth Games, he said yes straight away. He couldn't wait to represent his borough and lead them to the trophy.

'Welcome to the team,' one of the coaches, Ahmet Akdag, said with a smile. 'With you and Reiss together in attack, we've got a great chance of winning!'

Reiss? Reiss Nelson?! While Jadon had never met him before, he had heard a lot about him. Every young footballer in Southwark knew about Reiss because a) he was a brilliant winger and b) he was already at the Arsenal academy. According to a lot of the local kids, Jadon and Reiss were rivals for the title of 'Best Young Player in South London', but now they would be playing together in the same Southwark team!

'Hey, I'm Jadon – nice to meet you,' he introduced himself humbly at the first training session.

'Don't worry, I know who you are!' Reiss laughed. 'Nice to meet you too at last. You ready to win this competition?'

'Yes, let's goooooo, bro!'

There were other talented academy players at the Southwark training session that day, but Jadon and Reiss were miles ahead of everyone else, in an elite league of their own. The two of them raced around the pitch, scoring goals and pulling off outrageous skills, while making everything look so effortless and elegant.

'Woah, these kids are incredible!' Akdag was soon saying excitedly to his fellow coach, Sayce Holmes-Lewis. It didn't take a scouting genius to see that these young Southwark stars were both going to become professional players when they were older.

Jadon and Reiss quickly became close friends off the pitch, which made them even more unstoppable on the pitch. Soon, they knew each other's games so well that they could predict where the other would be and what run they would make.

'Cheers, J – what a ball!'

Jadon also loved testing himself against Reiss in training. The challenge was on to be the best player on the pitch...

...Who could dribble past the most opponents?

...Who could pick out the perfect pass?

...And who could score the greatest goal?

With their fun, friendly football rivalry, they inspired each other to improve.

Once the London Youth Games started at the Crystal Palace National Sports Centre, however, it wasn't Jadon vs Reiss anymore; it was Jadon and Reiss. As well as sublime talent, the two boys also shared a fierce determination to succeed, and together, they destroyed defence after defence with their speed, skill and teamwork. They won every single one of their ten games, scoring twenty-four goals between them, until eventually the trophy was theirs.

Southwark! Southwark! Southwark!

They had done it; out of all its thirty-two boroughs, they were the Champions of London! With their arms around each other's shoulders and winners' medals around their necks, Jadon and Reiss stood with their teammates, smiling for the cameras. The future was bright; the future was theirs.

After the competition, the young stars of South London went back to their different academies, but now that they were best friends, they often met up to play in local games together. On the caged pitches of Kennington, the big debate continued:

'Jadon or Reiss – who's better?'

'Jadon and Reiss, battle each other!'

At first, they usually accepted the challenge and entertained the crowd, but after a while, Jadon and Reiss decided that it was time to stop. What was the point in competing? They were football friends, not football rivals, and they wanted to help, not hurt, each other. The future was theirs together. They were both brilliant footballers and they were both going to become superstars, in South London and beyond.

CHAPTER 6

LEAVING SOUTH LONDON

'Boarding school?'

When he first heard those two words at the family dinner table, Jadon was only ten years old, and he spat them back out as if they tasted bad. Why on earth would he want to leave all his mates in South London behind and go away to boarding school? It sounded so posh and boring!

The situation wasn't quite that simple, however. Watford were offering to pay for everything, and Jadon's parents thought it was a good idea.

'Look, we know you don't want to leave home,' his dad explained, 'but this is an amazing opportunity for you to get a great education, and to get away from here too.'

'I love it here, though!' Jadon wanted to argue back, but he understood what his dad was trying to say. While he had lots of fun playing street football in Kennington, there was also a darker side to living in the area. For a young kid like Jadon, there were a lot of bad influences and distractions around, and the older he got, the more he might be tempted to do the wrong thing and throw away all of his hard work, effort and talent.

'Okay, fine, I'll do it,' Jadon agreed eventually. For the sake of his professional football dream, he would leave South London and give boarding school a go.

Arriving at the Harefield Academy, however, turned out to be like his early experiences at Watford all over again. Arggh, where was he supposed to go and what was he supposed to do? It was like a totally different world! Jadon was so used to his old street football mates in Kennington that he had forgotten how to speak to new people. What should he say?

At first, he found it really tough being so far from home with no friends to talk to. He felt like the odd one out, like he didn't fit in at all, and he kept getting into trouble with his teachers. Had he made a terrible mistake?

'I want to come back – pleeeeaaaaaasssssse!' Jadon begged his parents tearfully on the phone.

'I know it's hard, son, but you've got to keep going,' his mum replied, trying her best to reassure him. It was really upsetting to hear Jadon sounding so sad and lonely, but she was sure that he was in the best possible place for his long-term future.

'Okay, Mum.' It took a while, but eventually Jadon calmed down and accepted his situation, after a wake-up call from his Watford coaches.

'Look, you're in danger of wasting an amazing opportunity here,' they warned him at the start of Year 8. 'If you don't improve your attitude and your behaviour at school, we'll have to release you from the academy.'

Woah no, he couldn't let that happen! Although Jadon still didn't feel at home at the Harefield Academy, he tried to concentrate on the positives. Not only was boarding school helping him to grow up fast, but it was also allowing him to focus firmly on his favourite thing: football.

Each day at Harefield, Jadon was allowed to leave his morning classes early to go and train with the Watford academy. Then, when school finished, he stayed behind to make up for the lost lesson time before going back for an evening football session. Brilliant, maybe being at boarding school was better than being at a state school in South London after all!

Following a difficult first year at Harefield, Jadon began to turn things around. He stopped being naughty at school because he was fully committed to football now. He understood that it wasn't just about having fun anymore – it was also about working towards a brighter future, for him and his family. The more time he spent practising his skills, the more he began to stand out above the rest at the Watford academy.

When they travelled to Ireland to compete in the 2012 Mayo International Cup, the team didn't win the overall trophy, but Jadon returned home with the Golden Boot award. Yes, he was still small compared to most of the other kids, but he was blessed with a magic touch, the special talent to make the game look so effortless and elegant. The kid could do it all – skills, dribbling, passing, shooting – while running rings around everyone else. And he had the self-confidence of a superstar too.

'What's your dream?' Louis Lancaster, the youth coach, asked his players one day. After some time to think, most came back with the answer 'to play for the Watford first-team', while others said 'to become a professional footballer'. Jadon, however, was aiming a lot higher than that, even at the age of fourteen.

'I want to play for one of Europe's top clubs,' he said with a very serious look on his face, 'and I want to represent my country and make my family proud.'

But while Jadon's aims sounded very ambitious, Lancaster didn't doubt for a moment that the boy could do it.

CHAPTER 7

THE ROCKET AND THE NEW RONALDINHO

'Jadon, it's time to get off YouTube now please,' the teacher called out across the computer room, and not for the first time at the Harefield Academy. 'Come on, you've got proper schoolwork to do.'

'Yes, Miss,' he replied, but after waiting a minute, the video site was back up on his screen. What was it that Jadon was so desperate to keep watching? Fantastic football skills compilations, of course, featuring one player in particular: Ronaldinho!

The Brazilian forward was Jadon's number one hero, his favourite footballer in the world. Why? Well, for lots of reasons, but there were three really big ones:

43

1) For Ronaldinho, football was all about having fun and he always played the game with a grin on his face.

In one of Jadon's favourite videos, the Brazilian showed off his ball-juggling skills and did lots of tricks on his way out onto the training pitch. Ronaldinho didn't need to do it; he did it because he wanted to, because he just loved football and enjoying himself.

'That's what I want to do too,' Jadon decided. From that day on, hardly a moment went by when he didn't have a ball at his feet. Even when the Watford coaches were talking to them about team tactics, Jadon would be standing there while still juggling the ball.

2) Whenever he watched Ronaldinho play, he always saw a piece of skill that made him say, 'Woah!'

Jadon was too young to have watched him play live during his glory days at Barcelona, but he was still starring for AC Milan, and besides, old clips was what YouTube was for! Ronaldinho's highlight reels were by far the best on the internet. While his goals were great, his skills were even better:

The famous flip flaps,

The sombrero flicks,

The croqueta taps,

The Samba dance moves,

The chest juggles,

The backheel nutmegs,

The no-look passes,

The rabona crosses...

The list went on and on – unbelievable! Ronaldinho could make even top defenders look like fools, and he could do things with the ball that Jadon had never seen before. 'Woah, how did he do that? I definitely need to learn that one!' he marvelled. Every day was a school day, although not necessarily in the way that his teachers at Harefield intended.

3) But despite all the skills, what Jadon really admired most about Ronaldinho was his confidence.

It was one thing doing those cool tricks in training, but doing them at full speed under pressure in proper football matches? Wow, that took real courage as well as talent! The Brazilian forward played football in the best possible way – with fun, fearlessness, freedom, and flair.

'That's what I want to do too,' Jadon decided. For

now, he was only interested in one thing: attacking. He just wanted to score and create as many goals as possible for his team, while at the same time making people say 'Woah!' with his skills. For Jadon, that was what football was all about.

By then, Watford had already moved him up to play for the Under-15s, the year group above his own. The jump might have scared some youngsters, but not Jadon, or 'The Rocket' as his coaches had started calling him because of his rapid runs. Nothing fazed him when it came to football. So what if he wasn't as big and strong as his opponents? He was used to that from his days at Blue Park. No problem – he would just have to work hard to become even quicker and more skilful, so that he could skip past them before they knocked him off the ball! 'The Rocket' was ready to take off, on the next step in his journey to becoming a top professional player.

'Come on, I can do this!' he told himself with total self-belief, and before long, he was dribbling past the older boys as easily as ever. Progress!

During their training sessions, Lancaster made

sure to give Jadon lots of positive feedback and encouragement, but he also tried to test him as much as possible.

'Go on, Jadon,' the coach said, 'let's see what you can do when your team has fewer players.'

Challenge accepted! The training match started out as 9 vs 7, then moved on to 10 vs 6, and yet still he was able to stand out as one of the best players on the pitch.

'Great work, Jadon – what a pass!'

After only a few weeks with the Under-15s, Jadon was back to making football look effortless and elegant again. When he got the ball, he wasn't interested in taking the safe, simple option; no, he always took the exciting, skilful option instead. Inspired by his hero Ronaldinho, he had the courage to keep trying out new tricks, plus the self-confidence to step up and shine when it mattered most. He always seemed to find a way to raise his game for the big pressure moments, whether it was his coach calling, 'Next Goal Wins!' in training, or the final minutes of a proper important match.

At that time, Watford were a Category Three academy, which meant that most of the time they played against lower league teams. At least once a year, however, they got to take on the mighty Arsenal, and in their biggest game of the season, who produced a moment of brilliance to win the match? Jadon, of course! With the score at 1–1, he got the ball on the halfway line, and then turned and glided past two Arsenal defenders with ease.

Go on, J, SCORE!

He still had work to do, but 'The Rocket' was in no rush. He dribbled into the penalty area like he had all the time in the world, and then fired an unstoppable shot into the top corner. 2–1!

Goooooooooooooooooooooaaaaaaaaaaaaaaaaalllllllllllllll llllllllllll!!!!!!!!!!!!!!!!!!!

What a solo strike from Watford's young superstar! Jadon was getting better and better, and the big clubs were beginning to notice him.

CHAPTER 8

MOVING TO MANCHESTER CITY

As a football scout for Manchester City, Joe Shields's task was to discover the top young players in the south of England. Unfortunately, a lot of them had already been signed up by Chelsea, but there were still a few future stars playing for other, smaller London clubs, and Shields was sure that he had found one. Yes, after almost a year of watching the boy play, the 'Woah!' moment had finally arrived.

'There's this kid at Watford called Jadon Sancho,' he reported back to his bosses at the City academy eagerly, 'and I think he's a really special talent. You should have seen the goal he scored today, and against Arsenal too!'

Shields knew what the first question would be, so he decided to answer it before it was even asked. 'So far, none of the other big clubs seem to be watching him, but they soon will.'

Interesting! City's next step was to send more scouts to watch Jadon in action, and they all agreed with Shields's original opinion – yes, he was a very special talent, and the longer they waited, the more likely it was that Chelsea or Arsenal would offer him a contract first.

'Right, let's get him now then!' the City academy coaches decided, as Jadon's fifteenth birthday approached.

Once he heard that Manchester City wanted to sign him, Jadon's mind was made up immediately: of course he wanted to go there! The club was on a big-money mission to become one of the best in Europe, and with stars like Sergio Agüero, Vincent Kompany, David Silva and Yaya Touré, they had already won two Premier League titles. Now, City were also looking to build the most successful academy in the country.

'And we want you to be a big part of it,' they told

Jadon.

How exciting! It was an offer he couldn't refuse, and an opportunity he couldn't waste. In order to follow his professional football dream, Jadon didn't mind moving all the way from the south of England to the north. After years at the Harefield Academy, Jadon was used to living away from home anyway. And while he would always be grateful for Watford's support, it felt like the right time for him to move on to a new challenge.

'Let's go!' Jadon told his parents.

It was only when he arrived at his first training session for the Manchester City Under-16s, however, that he realised how much hard work lay ahead of him. Jadon might have been one of the youngest players there, and going from a Category Three to a Category One academy was a big jump to make, but wow, these kids were incredible! He was no longer the best player like he had been at Watford every week. In fact, Jadon had gone all the way from the top to the bottom because not only were the young City players highly skilful, but they were also a lot stronger and quicker than him.

'Unlucky, keep going!' the Under-16 coaches encouraged him when he lost the ball.

Right – Jadon had some serious catching up to do if he wanted to compete with the most promising young players at Manchester City, but that was okay. He believed in himself, and he was ready and willing to work as hard as he could in training to become the best again.

'Great effort, well done!' those same coaches were soon shouting.

Onto the next challenge: Jadon definitely had the talent and the determination, but did he really have the speed to skip past defenders at the highest level? Some people at City had their doubts, but Jadon was happy to prove them wrong. Besides, with his quick feet and clever body swerves, he could beat his opponents in other ways, as he showed on his Under-16s debut against Birmingham City by scoring five goals.

'Wow, this boy really is a bit special!' The manager Gareth Taylor smiled to himself.

One great game was only the beginning, though. If he wanted to succeed at a massive club like Manchester City, Jadon would have to play well consistently, week-in week-out. The club wanted to win every single game at every single level. No problem! In his first year with the Under-16s, they went the whole season unbeaten, and what a team they were! With Jadon creating chances on one wing, and Luke Bolton doing the same on the other, they were unstoppable, scoring goal after goal.

'Look out Premier League, here we come!' Jadon called out with cheeky confidence as he celebrated with his teammates.

By April 2016, his impressive performances had caught the attention of Jason Wilcox, the coach of the City Under-18s, who named Jadon as a substitute for their big FA Youth Cup final against a Chelsea team featuring Mason Mount and Tammy Abraham.

Wow, what an amazing opportunity for a 16-year-old – Jadon couldn't wait! In the first leg in Manchester, he only came on for the final few minutes, but in the second leg at Stamford Bridge,

City were losing early in the second half, so Wilcox sent him on much sooner.

Could Jadon use his skills to save the day for his team? Unfortunately not, but he did manage to make an impact by setting up a late consolation goal for Brahim Díaz. This time, City finished as FA Youth Cup runners-up, but Jadon was determined to help lead them to the trophy next year.

'And I'll be a starter by then, not a sub!'

Jadon was off to a stunning start at City, but with so many other talented young footballers around him at the academy, there was no time for him to rest and get too comfortable. They were all competing for the same precious prize – a spot in Pep Guardiola's senior squad one day soon.

So, ahead of the 2016–17 season, Jadon set himself some new and even more ambitious goals:

Winning the FA Youth Cup with the Under-18s,

Getting some game-time for the Under-23s,

And the biggest of all, training with the Manchester City first team.

CHAPTER 9

COMPETING TO BE THE BEST

From the very first day of pre-season training, Jadon was determined to stand out above the rest of Manchester City's young stars. He wasn't the only one, though; a creative midfielder called Phil Foden shared that same winning mentality. Every day, they battled to be the best at everything: skills, drills, one-v-ones, rondo and passing games, shooting practice, even fitness challenges.

'Okay, let's stop together,' Jadon and Phil agreed eventually, once they were the last players left running in the beep test.

All that tiring work was totally worth it because both players started the new season on fire. In the

Under-18s Premier League, Jadon scored against West Brom and Everton, while Phil scored two as City thrashed Liverpool 7–0. Soon after, it was time for their biggest game of the year – the Manchester derby against United. With the pressure on, City's stars shone brightest. Jadon set up the first goal for Luke and then Phil scored the second. 2–0!

'Mate, we did it – Manchester is blue!' Jadon cheered as they celebrated the win together.

The City Under-18s were still unbeaten, and their winning run continued with a comfortable victory away at Sunderland. Jadon was the star of the show again, with goals, an assist, and a series of entertaining runs to rival even his hero Ronaldinho.

Collecting the ball on the left side of the box, Jadon did a Cruyff-turn to escape from his marker and then cut inside with a flash of quick feet. Woah! What next? With no teammates in the middle waiting for the cross, he went for glory himself, curling a shot into the bottom corner. *4–0!*

Gooooooooooooooooooooaaaaaaaaaaaaaaaaaalllllllllllllll llllllllllll!!!!!!!!!!!!!!!!!!!!

WOAH! It was a stunning bit of skill, inspired by his days at Blue Park. It deserved a special celebration, but no, with a smile and a quick fist-pump, Jadon jogged back to the halfway line to carry on playing. At the age of sixteen, he was making Under-18s football look so easy.

Too easy, in fact; it was already time for Jadon to take on a new, tougher challenge. After destroying defences in England, could he do the same in Europe, for the City Under-19s in the UEFA Youth League? No problem! On his debut, he came off the bench to score against the German club Borussia Mönchengladbach, and then he headed home an important equaliser against the Scottish giants Celtic.

'Get in!' Jadon yelled, punching the air with more passion this time.

Eventually, RB Salzburg knocked City out of the competition on penalties, but who stepped up courageously and scored in the shoot-out? Yes, Jadon! Pressure, what pressure? He was fearless when it came to football.

'Let me take one,' he told his manager, Simon

Davies. 'I've got this.'

Davies was amazed by Jadon's bravery and brilliance, and he wasn't the only one. The City first-team manager, Pep Guardiola, was so impressed that he invited Jadon to join in with a senior training session.

Yessssss – another of his goals achieved! Jadon couldn't believe that he was actually passing the ball to Kevin De Bruyne, or trying to dribble past Vincent Kompany, but he didn't let that affect his focus or his self-belief. He deserved to be there, competing with the best players at the club, and this was his chance to show it.

'Moment I'll never forget!' Jadon posted afterwards on social media, alongside a photo of him talking to Guardiola, one of the best managers in the world.

What a sensational season he was having:

Twelve goals in fourteen games for the Under-18s,

Two in six for the Under-19s,

And now training with the first team!

But Jadon's break-out year was about to get even busier. In January 2017, the City youth coaches decided that it was time for Jadon to test himself at a higher level: the Under-23s.

Really, was he ready for that? He would be up against defenders who were much bigger and stronger than him, and older too. In the Premier League 2, teams were allowed to field three players above the age of twenty-three, and Jadon was still only sixteen!

But once again, he showed he had the talent and self-confidence to step up and shine. In just his second game, Jadon scored City's first goal and then set up the other in a 2–2 draw with Tottenham.

'Woah, what a performance!' the captain, Cameron Humphreys, congratulated him at the final whistle. 'Welcome to our team!'

Jadon enjoyed proving that he was good enough – and old enough – to shine at any level. He was on the best form of his life and he followed that up with strikes against Sunderland and Everton to make it three goals in five games for the Under-23s.

Next up: Arsenal, and his best friend Reiss! Although the match ended in a 3–3 draw, it was Reiss who won their friendly battle by grabbing a goal and an assist. But after the final whistle, they stood together as brothers, with their arms around each other's shoulders. Six years after leading Southwark to victory, the young stars of South London were still shining brightly, and the future was still theirs.

Jadon's amazing season was almost over, but first, he had one last goal to achieve – lifting the FA Youth Cup with the Under-18s. Winning a trophy would be the perfect way to end! With two goals each from Jadon and Phil, Manchester City had made it back to the final again, beating Southampton, Aston Villa and Stoke City along the way. Now, for the big one – the rematch against last year's champions, Chelsea.

'Come on, we can win this!' the City coach, Lee Carsley, encouraged them. Their team was packed with even better players this time around. In attack, Brahim and Lukas Nmecha were both back, alongside two new starters: Jadon and Phil!

'Let's goooooooo!'

Chelsea took the lead in the first leg in Manchester, but City battled their way back into the game. Midway through the second half, Jadon won the ball on the left wing and passed it quickly through to Phil, who dribbled into the box and scored. *1–1!*

'Yesssssssssss. Game on!'

In the second leg at Stamford Bridge, however, Chelsea were just too strong for them. Jadon could only watch and groan in frustration as they scored goal after goal. *2–1, 3–1, 4–1...*

'Noooo!' he thought as his shoulders slumped. 'We're going to be runners up *AGAIN!'*

With fifteen minutes still to go in the FA Youth Cup final, Jadon's manager decided to take him off. It was a disappointing way to end his season with City, but he preferred to focus on the positives, and there had been lots and lots of those. From the Under-18s, to the 19s, to the 23s, to training with the first team – Jadon had stepped up and proved himself again and again. And hopefully, there would be more special moments to come that summer with the England Under-17s.

CHAPTER 10

YOUNG LIONS:
PART I

The year 2017 – what a busy one it was for Steve
Cooper's England Under-17s. The Young Lions had
already taken part in the Algarve Tournament in
February and next up in May was the European
Championships in Croatia.

Jadon couldn't wait to join up with the squad again.
He was always proud to represent his country and
the Under-17s group knew each other so well that
they were like one big happy family. So what if Marc
Guéhi and Callum Hudson-Odoi had just beaten Jadon
and Phil in the FA Youth Cup final? This wasn't club
football anymore; they were all on the same team,
working together to win the same trophy.

England had only ever won the Under-17s Euros twice before:

In 2010, with Conor Coady and Ross Barkley,

And in 2014, with Joe Gomez and Dominic Solanke.

So, could Jadon and co. become the third team to triumph? That was the plan! People were already talking about them as England's new 'golden generation'. In particular, the front four players were packed with such exciting talent:

Phil in attacking midfield,

Jadon on the left,

Callum on the right,

And Rhian Brewster as the central striker.

Wow – with a line-up like that it was easy to see why England were one of the favourites to win the tournament! After a fun training camp, the players were feeling very confident – a little too confident perhaps. Because in their first group game against Erling Haaland's Norway, they found themselves 1–0 down after just seven minutes. Uh-oh!

It was a bad start, but the England players didn't

panic. Instead, they pushed forward on the attack.
Just two minutes later, Jadon dribbled all the way from
the halfway line to the Norway penalty area, leaving
three defenders trailing behind. After a heavy touch, it
looked like he was going to lose the ball, but no, Jadon
skipped past the last defender and then rounded the
keeper with a sublime bit of skill.

Wow! Now, for the finish... The angle was too tight
for Jadon to shoot himself, so he crossed the ball to
Rhian for a tap-in. *1–1!*

'Yesssss!' Rhian screamed, running straight over to
Jadon, but he wasn't in the mood for celebrating. Not
yet – England weren't winning. So instead, he grabbed
the ball out of the net and ran back for the restart.

'Let's goooooooo!'

After Jadon's moment of magic, England cruised to
victory. Callum set up Rhian for his second goal, and
then Phil made it three. Game over! On to the next...

Jadon had been England's star player against
Norway, and he was even better against Ukraine.
With his silky skills and body swerves, he terrorised
their poor right-back all game long. And after setting

up two more goals for George McEachran and Rhian, Jadon finally grabbed one of his own. Following a neat one-two with Phil, his first shot struck the post, but he fired in the rebound. *3–0!*

Goooooooooooooooooooooaaaaaaaaaaaaaaaallllllllllllll llllllllllll!!!!!!!!!!!!!!!!!!!!!

A cheeky smile spread across Jordan's face as Rhian rushed over to him. Yes, it was safe for them to celebrate this time!

Two games, two wins – so far, so good for England. And to cap off an incredible group stage, Jadon scored a double against the Netherlands. Wow, he had three goals and three assists already!

Now that they were through to the knock-out stage, however, things were about to get a lot harder. In the quarter-finals, Ireland defended fiercely and made it really difficult for England's attackers. One more moment of Jadon magic, however, was enough to win the match. From thirty yards out, he unleashed a stunning strike that flew into the top corner. *1–0!*

Goooooooooooooooooooooaaaaaaaaaaaaaaaallllllllllllll llllllllllll!!!!!!!!!!!!!!!!!!!!!

As he raced away to celebrate, Jadon cheekily put a finger to his lips. 'Shhhhhhhhh!' He was on fire for England, and they were through to the semi-finals to face…

Turkey! Although they didn't have many famous stars in their team, the Young Lions couldn't afford to underestimate them. Turkey had already surprised Italy and Croatia in the group stage, and they would do the same to England if they weren't careful.

Jadon knew what he had to do, and he was ready to shine for his country again. In the tenth minute, he intercepted a pass on the left and raced forward with the ball. Three Turkey defenders quickly surrounded him as England's danger man, so Jadon slid a no-look pass through to Callum, who whipped a shot into the top corner. *1–0!*

'Thanks J, what a ball!'

Callum almost returned the favour in the thirty-first minute, but Jadon's shot was saved by the keeper. So close! Never mind, he was playing so well that he would surely get another chance…

As Phil looked up to play a pass, he could see six

red Turkey shirts around him, but not a single white shirt. Where were his teammates when he needed them? Oh wait – suddenly he spotted Jadon to his left; he was on the move! From their years together at the City academy, Phil knew exactly what to do. *PING!* He slid an inch-perfect pass in between two Turkey defenders, and into the space that Jadon was sprinting towards...

Should he shoot first time? No, Jadon decided to take a touch to steady himself, before curling the ball into the far bottom corner. *2–0!*

Goooooooooooooooooooaaaaaaaaaaaaaaaaalllllllllllllll llllllllllllll!!!!!!!!!!!!!!!!!!!

As he jogged over to the corner flag, Jadon threw his arms out wide like a superstar. It wasn't the flashiest of his five goals at the tournament, but he knew how important it was for his team.

'Yessssssssss!' Phil yelled as he jumped on Jadon's back.

Eventually, the final whistle blew, and the news was official: England were through to the Euros final! Now, if they could just beat Spain, they would be the champions, and the trophy would be theirs.

The pressure was on, but the Young Lions began the final confidently, like it was any other game. In the eighteenth minute, Jadon got the ball, spun it beautifully and passed it forward to Callum, who did exactly what he'd done against Turkey: whip a shot into the top corner. *1–0 to England!*

What a start! Spain, however, bounced back, not once but twice.

Mateu Morey finished off a flowing team move. *1–1!*

Phil hit a long-range rocket that fizzed into the bottom corner. *2–1 to England!*

Then, in the last seconds of the final, Nacho Díaz headed the ball in. *2–2!*

Noooooooooooo! It was a devastating blow for England because not only was the final now going to penalties, but Cooper had just subbed off Jadon and Phil, two of his best penalty takers! Instead of stepping up, they had to watch from the sidelines as Rhian and then Joel Latibeaudiere missed their spot-kicks for the national team. Spain, not England, were the new

Under-17 Champions of Europe.

NOOOOOOOOO! Jadon sat there for a long time staring down at the grass below his boots. In that awful moment, not even his winning the tournament's Golden Player award could make the loss any less painful. He had worked so hard and performed so well in every match, grabbing five goals and five assists, but in the end, it was another defeat in another final.

'Absolutely gutted,' Jadon wrote on social media later that night. 'But I must say I am truly honoured and proud to be a part of such an amazing squad!'

Fortunately, the busy year for the England Under-17s wasn't over yet. No, they still had one more chance to win a major trophy – at the Under-17s World Cup in October. Jadon and his teammates were already counting down the days.

CHAPTER 11

GOING TO GERMANY

Good news – that's what Jadon wanted to hear, to cheer him up after England's Euro final defeat to Spain. And just days after returning home from Croatia, it arrived:

'We have three or four players we genuinely believe have a very good chance of making it to the first team,' the Manchester City chairman, Khaldoon Al Mubarak, announced to the world. 'You look at Sancho, you look at Phil Foden, you look at Brahim Díaz… these are players that are extremely talented.'

Yessss, it was official – Jadon was one of City's three most promising young players! Together, they posed for photos in the club's new home shirt and spent an unforgettable summer training with Guardiola's senior squad.

'3 young boys all following 1 dream,' Jadon posted on social media with a happy picture of him, Phil and Brahim joking around after practice.

During practice, however, they stayed fully focused on football. It was a fantastic opportunity to impress the City manager and Jadon was determined to make the most of every moment. How? By believing in himself and showing the best of his ability.

'Come on, I can do this,' he told himself before training every day.

With his wide smiles and wonderful skills, Jadon soon made lots of new friends in the City first team. When he needed to, though, he didn't mind making them look like fools on the football pitch. In fact, he loved it. Using one of his favourite body swerves, Jadon faked to dribble left but at the last second went right instead, leaving Raheem Sterling frozen in shock.

'Woah!' the other City players cheered. 'Are you alright, Raz? The kid's really embarrassed you there!'

But rather than looking angry, Raheem just looked

amazed. 'You're going to be a big player,' he told Jadon, with a nod of respect. 'Keep working hard.'

Wow, what a thing to hear from one of your heroes! Of all the senior stars at City, Raheem was the one that Jadon looked up to the most. That was because they were both speedy, skilful wingers, but also because they shared a very similar history. They had both grown up playing street football in London, before rising through the ranks at smaller clubs – QPR and Watford – and then signing for top Premier League teams: Liverpool and Manchester City.

So far, so similar, but Raheem had gone on to make his senior debut at the age of just seventeen, and Jadon was desperate to do the same. Why not? Why wait? After his Golden Player performance for England at the Euros, he felt ready for the challenge of first team football. His best friend Reiss had already made his debut for Arsenal, and they were the same age. Jadon's argument had always been that if he was good enough, then he was old enough.

But did City feel the same way? That was the big question, and Jadon wanted to know the answer before he signed a new contract at the club. Raheem, Sergio Agüero, Leroy Sané, Gabriel Jesus, Kevin De Bruyne, Bernardo Silva, David Silva – there were already so many world-class attackers ahead of him in the first team squad! Jadon was willing to keep working hard and earn his opportunities, but if he was hardly ever going to play, no matter what, then what was the point in wasting his time sitting on the bench?

Jadon and his family had several meetings with Guardiola, but they never got the answer they were hoping for. Unfortunately, the City manager couldn't make any promises about the amount of football Jadon would play that season, pointing out that he was still young and that he would just have to be patient, like Phil and Brahim.

Jadon was disappointed, but at least now he knew the full situation. While the club believed in his ability, they saw him as a star for the future, not the present. If he wanted to play more first-team football straight away, he would just have to move on.

'Okay, well if City can't guarantee me game-time, then which club can?' Jadon wondered.

Arsenal and Tottenham both tried to bring him back to London, but City didn't want to sell their young star to one of their Premier League rivals. There was also talk of signing for one of the Spanish giants, Real Madrid or Barcelona. However, in the end, it was another European country that attracted Jadon the most.

'What about going to Germany?' his agent asked. 'Borussia Dortmund are also interested in you.'

Sure, why not?! Jadon had already handled leaving London to move to Manchester, so maybe he could take another step and travel to a different country, in order to play first-team football.

At that time, Jadon didn't know very much about Dortmund, but he did know two things:

1) They were a very good team on FIFA, with Pierre-Emerick Aubameyang and Marco Reus in attack!

2) The club was famous for giving their young players a chance. Reus had been starring for the first team since the age of twenty, while Mario Götze and Christian Pulisic had both made their debuts as seventeen-year-olds.

Seventeen – the same age as Jadon! The more he heard about Dortmund, the more it felt like the right place for him. After talking to the club's coaches, he could see the path ahead of him: a few months in the Under-23s to adapt, and then up to the first team as soon as possible. Their latest wonderkid, Ousmane Dembélé, had just moved to Barcelona for more than £100 million, and so the club were looking for a new wing wizard to replace him. They were even willing to give Jadon a starting shirt number straight away. Which did he prefer – 7 or 9?

That was it – Jadon's mind was made up. 'I'm more of a winger than a striker, so I'll take 7 please. Right, let's do this!'

For just £8 million, Jadon became a Dortmund player. He knew that it wasn't going to be easy, living in a new country, learning a new language, and fighting for a first-team spot with the likes of Reus, Aubameyang, Pulisic, Shinji Kagawa and Andriy Yarmolenko. Some people told him it was a big risk to take, but Jadon always had the confidence and courage to try something different. 'If you believe, you can achieve' – that was his motto in life.

'It was a difficult decision,' he wrote in a thank-you message to everyone at Manchester City, 'but the time is right for a new challenge where I can start to fulfil my potential.'

CHAPTER 12

YOUNG LIONS: PART II

The very next day, Jadon posted a picture of himself holding up a yellow-and-black shirt with '7 SANCHO' on the back.

'Happy to be a Borussia Dortmund Player!! Time to Work', the caption read.

It was the start of a brave new adventure for Jadon, but with a chef to cook his meals, his dad to keep him company, and a teacher to give him German lessons, he was free to focus on his main goal: becoming a first-team footballer.

During the week, Jadon mostly trained with the Dortmund senior squad, but the coaches decided that he wasn't quite ready for competitive matches at that level yet. Yes, he was brilliant on the ball, especially in one-v-one situations, but his work off the ball would need to be better. In Germany, teams pressed hard from the front, and even attackers had to learn to track back and defend. So, Jadon started off playing for the Under-19s and then the Under-23s, getting more and more game-time every weekend. First fifty minutes, then sixty, then seventy...

'That's it – well done, Jadon!' cheered the Under-23s manager, Jan Siewert, after an amazing assist against SV Rödinghausen.

Just as Jadon was beginning to get used to German football, however, he headed off on another journey – to the Under-17s World Cup in India.

Dortmund had asked him to stay and miss the tournament, but there was no way that Jadon could say no to England. His band of brothers needed him! The Young Lions should have won the Euros final back in May, but that heartbreak had made them even more determined to lift the trophy this time, on an even bigger stage. If they succeeded, they would become the first England team to ever win the

Under-17 World Cup!

So in the end, Jadon and his club had come to an agreement: he would go and play for England in their three group games, and after that, he would return to Germany. Deal! He would just have to make the most of every match...

In only the fifth minute against Chile, Jadon dribbled in between two defenders and threaded a pass through to Callum. *1–0!*

Early in the second half, Jadon pounced on a mistake by the keeper and calmly tapped into an empty net. *2–0!*

Then ten minutes later, he collected a pass from George McEachran and coolly swept the ball into the bottom corner. *3–0!*

'Yesssss!' Jadon yelled as he jumped up and punched the air. What a start – he already had two goals and an assist!

And after crushing Chile, Jadon moved on to Mexico. As he got the ball out on the left wing, he had two defenders in front of him, but with a sudden skip to the right, Jadon somehow managed to escape.

First, he played a one-two with Angel Gomes, and then he set up Phil for the shot. *2–0!*

A few minutes later, Jadon danced his way into the Mexico box again, fooling three defenders with his quick feet, fakes and body swerves. When he ran out of room, he tried to cross it to Rhian in the middle, but the ball struck a defender on the arm before it reached him. Penalty!

With a puff of his cheeks, Jadon jogged forward and sent the keeper the wrong way. *3–0!*

Goooooooooooooooooooooaaaaaaaaaaaaaaaaalllllllllllllll lllllllllllll!!!!!!!!!!!!!!!!!!!!

Another game, another goal, and another assist. What a superstar – Jadon was on fire! But after one more win against Iraq, sadly it was time for him to wave goodbye to the Under-17s World Cup and go back to Germany. Already? Oh well…

'Good luck!' Jadon told his teammates. 'Go win it without me!'

That wasn't going to be easy, though. A few days later, while Jadon was back scoring for the Dortmund Under-19s in the UEFA Youth League, the England

Under-17s were struggling against Japan in the Round of 16. Where was their big game Golden Player when they needed him? The match finished 0–0, but fortunately, they won the penalty shoot-out. Phew!

'COME ON ENGLAND. Well done team!' Jadon cheered his friends on from home.

After that nerve-wracking experience, the Young Lions grew stronger and stronger, beating the USA 4–1 in the quarter-finals, and then Brazil 3–1 in the semi-finals. Hurray, they were through to the World Cup final!

Jadon was delighted for his teammates, but at the same time, he couldn't help feeling a bit jealous. It had been his dream to help England win the Under-17s World Cup, and now they were just one game away from achieving that aim without him. Plus, who were they playing in the final? Their old Euros enemies, Spain!

'I really wish I was still there,' Jadon moaned to himself. But never mind – with so many talented players in the squad, the Young Lions didn't really seem to miss him. Phil was creating magic in midfield, while Rhian had scored two stunning hat-tricks in a row.

'Good luck team!' Jadon posted on social media ahead of the big game. While England competed in the World Cup final, he would be taking on KFC Uerdingen with the Dortmund Under-23s – and he certainly knew which game he'd rather be playing in! As he sat in the dressing room ahead of kick-off, his mind was miles away in India. How were his England teammates feeling – excited? Nervous? Probably a bit of both… Noooo, he needed to concentrate on his own match, not theirs!

'Can I send a quick video message to my friends?' Jadon asked his manager eventually. 'They're in a final and I'm not there.'

Siewert nodded. 'Yes, but after that, I need you to focus fully on today's game. I know you're disappointed, but you're a professional and this is a great chance for you to prove yourself.'

'Yes, Boss!'

Although Dortmund lost 1–0, Jadon worked tirelessly for his team throughout, showing total commitment in both attack and defence.

'Well played,' Siewert said to Jadon when he was subbed off late in the second half. 'Now, go and find out how your friends are doing!'

The answer was... England were winning! From 2–0 down, the Young Lions had fought back brilliantly:

Rhian's header was too powerful to keep out. *2–1!*

Morgan Gibbs-White raced into the six-yard box to smash home Steven Sessegnon's cross. *2–2!*

Phil arrived at the back post to finish off a cross from Callum. *3–2!*

Marc reacted quickest in a goalmouth scramble. *4–2!*

And finally, Phil ran through and calmly slid his shot under the Spanish keeper. *5–2!*

What a win – England were the new Under-17 World Champions! As Jadon watched the wild scenes on TV, he felt a real sense of pride – for himself, but mainly for his band of football brothers. The Young Lions had achieved their dream, and although he sadly wasn't there to celebrate with them, he had still played his part.

'My team,' Jadon wrote on social media, followed by four big heart emojis.

CHAPTER 13

A RAPID
RISE

While Jadon really wished he could have won the Under-17s World Cup final with England, in the end things had worked out well for him. By returning to Dortmund and demonstrating his commitment to the club, he had impressed not only Siewert, but also the first-team manager, Dutch-born Peter Bosz.

'I think he's ready,' Bosz decided. 'Let's give him a chance in the Bundesliga.'

So, on the same day that England played their quarter-final against the USA, Jadon had made his professional debut at the age of seventeen. Just like he had always wanted!

With ten minutes to go, Dortmund were drawing

2–2 away at Eintracht Frankfurt, but they needed to win in order to stay top of the league above their rivals Bayern Munich. As Bosz turned to his bench to make an attacking substitution, he had so many options to choose from: Shinji, Andriy, Jacob Bruun Larsen, Alexander Isak… But no, the manager brought on Jadon instead.

Wow, what a massive moment! Although he felt nervous and scared, Jadon pushed those emotions to the back of his mind and focused on the positives instead: this was a huge opportunity for him, and he was ready to shine.

'When you get the ball,' Bosz told him as he waited on the touchline, 'just do what you do best – beat defenders and create chances.'

Jadon did exactly what his Dortmund manager asked him to do. As soon as he got the ball on the left wing, he ran forward and tried to take on the Frankfurt full-back. Unfortunately, his first dribble didn't go so well. Jadon thought he had lots of time to get his quick feet going, but no, in a flash, the flying full-back tackled him and sent him crashing to the floor. Owwwww!

It was a painful welcome to professional football, but Jadon got straight back up and tried again. The next time the ball came to him, he did everything a lot faster. After one touch to control, he played a swift pass to Mario Götze and then kept running for the one-two. What next? Jadon could see a midfielder racing in to close him down, but he was getting in the groove now. With two quick taps, he slid the ball through his opponent's legs and collected it on the other side.

MEGS! Jadon had come a long way since his days at Blue Park, but his love for skills was still the same.

In the end, Dortmund didn't get the winning goal they wanted, but Jadon was pretty pleased with his first ten-minute performance.

'Well played, J!' said Pierre-Emerick, putting an arm around his shoulder. The Dortmund captain had really helped him to settle in at his new club.

'Thanks, Auba – you too!'

Jadon hoped to get more game-time soon, and maybe even his first start. Unfortunately, it took another few months and a change of manager for that amazing day to arrive. In December 2017, Bosz left Dortmund and Peter Stöger became the new boss for the rest of the season. In their very first training session together, Stöger saw something special about Jadon and he decided that the young winger deserved a proper run in the team – not just a few minutes as a sub, but the whole ninety minutes.

'I want you to go out there and show the supporters what you can really do,' his new manager said.

'Thanks, Boss, I will!'

On 14 January 2018, Jadon got to play his first full game, in which Dortmund drew 0–0 with Wolfsburg, and five days later, he did it again as they drew 1–1 with Hertha Berlin. They weren't exactly the results that the team wanted, but Jadon was off to a really exciting start.

In the seventieth minute against Hertha, Jadon won the ball on the left wing and dribbled into the opponents' box at speed. Danger alert! After a couple of stepovers, he tried to cross it to Christian, but a defender blocked it. Never mind, Jadon got the ball back, looked up, and tried again. With a whip of his right foot, he chipped a curling cross towards the back post, where Shinji scored with a diving header. *1–1!*

Jadon had his first assist in professional football! There was no time for a proper celebration, but as the Dortmund players ran back for the restart, they gave him lots of hugs and high-fives. And after the final whistle, his manager was full of praise.

'Sancho is a really good lad who has pace and is good in one-on-ones,' Stöger said. 'If he continues developing the way he is, then he's got a great future ahead of him.'

After just three starts, Jadon won the Bundesliga's Rookie of the Month award. He was making a name for himself already, and suddenly Dortmund would need his magic even more, when Auba signed for Arsenal. Jadon was sad at the departure of one of his best friends at the club, but at the same time, it left a big gap in the team's attack. Could he be the one to step up and fill it? Yes, of course he could!

After a few weeks out with an ankle injury, Jadon returned to the Dortmund starting line-up for their home game against Top Four rivals Bayer Leverkusen. And what an impact he would make!

In the thirteenth minute, he collected a pass from Christian and calmly curled a shot into the bottom corner. *1–0!*

Goooooooooooooooooooooaaaaaaaaaaaaaaaaaallllllllllllllll llllllllllll!!!!!!!!!!!!!!!!!!!

Jadon had already experienced the amazing atmosphere created by the famous 'Yellow Wall', the 80,000 Dortmund fans at the Westfalenstadion. This, however, was something extra special. He had just scored his first goal for the club – his first goal ever as a professional footballer, in fact – and so as he kissed the badge on his shirt and leapt high into the air, the noise was all for him!

'Jadon…,' the voice on the loudspeaker began.

'SAAAAAAANCHO!' the crowd screamed back.

Wow, unbelievable! Jadon had genuine goosebumps as he jogged back to the halfway line. Right, what next? He was hungry for more, and so was the rest of Dortmund's dangerous attack.

Jadon to Christian, to Mario, to Marco. *2–0!*

It was a brilliant team move, and there was an even better goal to come. Manuel Akanji's long pass was a little behind Jadon as he raced up the left wing, but as the ball dropped, he controlled it beautifully with the outside of his bright orange right boot, and then set up Maximilian Philipp to score. *3–0!*

Woah, what a sublime bit of skill! With the freedom to express himself, Jadon was on fire, and there was still time for him to grab his second assist of the game. From the left side of the box, he chipped another curling cross towards the back post, where Marco was waiting. *4–0!*

One goal, two assists and the man of the match award – Jadon was making professional football look so effortless. And what a rapid rise it had been. In the space of just six months, he had gone from playing for the Dortmund Under-19s to starring for the first team.

'Bring on next season!' Jadon announced with his usual cheeky confidence.

CHAPTER 14

A CONSISTENT GAMECHANGER

The year 2018 had already been the best one of Jadon's life so far, and the second half was set to get even better. After finishing fourth in the Bundesliga, a whopping twenty-nine points behind the champions Bayern Munich, Dortmund had made several key signings over the summer:

Two new midfielders, Thomas Delaney and Axel Witsel,

A new striker, Paco Alcácer,

And perhaps most importantly of all, a new manager: the highly rated Swiss, Lucien Favre.

Like Stöger, Favre liked his team to play with freedom, especially in attack. And like Stöger, Favre also spotted Jadon's exciting potential straight away. With the ball at his feet, the youngster had something extra special about him – that rare superstar quality. But while Jadon's natural ability was astonishing, there were two things that the new Dortmund manager wanted him to work on to make him even better:

1) **Becoming more clinical.** Skill was a big part of Jadon's game, but at times, he needed to be more direct with the ball. While tricks were fun and entertaining, it was goals and assists that won football matches, as Dortmund's new striker often reminded him in training.

'HURRY UP AND PASS IT!' Paco called out as Jadon tried to dribble around a fourth defender in a row. The Spaniard was a fantastic finisher, but in order for him to score lots of goals, he needed good service from the attackers around him.

'Sorry, coming!' Jadon called back, before crossing the ball in.

2) **Becoming more consistent.** In order to become one of Dortmund's star players, Jadon would need to shine for the full ninety minutes, not just

fifteen or twenty minutes. Plus, he would also need to perform well in match after match, all season long. That was the mark of a true world-class superstar.

Challenges eagerly accepted! As a humble eighteen-year-old, Jadon understood that he still had lots to learn. That's why he had signed for Dortmund – because it was the perfect place to develop as a player. With so many top coaches and experienced professionals around him, like Marco, Mario, Paco and Axel, every day was a chance for him to mature and improve.

'Keep working, keep learning,' Jadon posted on social media during preseason training.

Soon, it was time for the 2018–19 season to begin. How would Jadon get on in his first full year in the Bundesliga? At first, Favre chose to use him as a second-half sub, but he was so successful that surely he couldn't stay on the bench for long. Jadon was doing something special in every single match:

He came on and set up Marco to score his hundreth goal against RB Leipzig. *ASSIST!*

With Dortmund heading for a draw, he fooled two

Frankfurt defenders with a fantastic Cruyff Turn and then crossed the ball to Marius Wolf. *ASSIST!*

Against Nuremberg, Jadon only got sixteen minutes, but that was still plenty of time for him to impress his manager. First, Jadon controlled Thomas's long pass beautifully and then calmly slid a shot past the keeper. *GOOOAAALLL!*

Then, three minutes later, Jadon was on the ball again, teasing the tired Nuremberg defence, before pulling it back for Julian Weigl to strike. *ASSIST!*

Woah – Jadon had played a part in four Dortmund goals already, and he'd only been on the pitch for a total of one hundred minutes! His manager had challenged him to become a more consistent gamechanger, and that's exactly what he was now.

But just in case Favre still wasn't convinced, Jadon put on his best super sub performance yet. As he ran onto the field, Dortmund were losing 2–1 to Leverkusen, with twenty minutes to go. What they needed was a gamechanger, and it only took Jadon one minute to get the job done.

ZOOM! From deep in his own half, Jadon

dribbled the ball forward at full speed, leaving three Leverkusen players trailing behind. As he crossed the halfway line, he passed inside to Marco and then continued his run up the right wing.

Jadon and Marco were good friends with a very special connection on the football pitch. Together, they just clicked. So, as they attacked, Marco knew exactly when to slide the ball through to Jadon, and Jadon knew exactly when to pass it back. *2–2!*

'Yesssssssss!' Marco yelled as he jumped into Jadon's arms in front of the fans.

Game on! Fifteen minutes later, Paco gave Dortmund the lead, and in injury time, he added a fourth, after another assist from Jadon. 4–2!

Dortmund's young super sub had saved the day again!

'Sancho is without doubt one of the most exciting players in Europe,' declared the club's Sporting Director Michael Zorc as they handed him a well-deserved new contract.

Jadon was really loving life in Dortmund. Most of the time, the city was a lot more chilled out than

London, but while there was a match on at the Westfalenstadion, it went absolutely football mad! For Jadon, it was a dream come true to play in front of 80,000 loud, passionate fans every week, no matter what the weather, and hear them chant his name.

SAAAAAAANCHO!
SAAAAAAANCHO!
SAAAAAAANCHO!

What next? Jadon was already changing game after game in less than thirty minutes, so what might he be able to achieve if he got to play the full ninety? That's what the Dortmund fans were wondering, and now so was the manager. There was only one way to find out...

In their next game against Augsburg, Jadon got his first league start of the season at last. Hurray! During the first half, he showed flashes of his brilliance, but sadly they didn't lead to any Dortmund goals. His exciting runs always ended in disappointment – a poor touch, a heavy pass, or a shot off target.

'Arghhh!' By half-time, Jadon was feeling very frustrated, but he kept trying until eventually he succeeded. In the second half, he raced up the right wing and this time, he delivered a perfect cross to Paco. *GOAL!*

'Thanks, what a ball!' the striker cheered as they high-fived.

Yessssss, Jadon was the gamechanger yet again!

Eventually, Dortmund won the match 4–3, which meant they stayed top of the table as the Bundesliga stopped for the international break. There was no time for Jadon to rest, however, because he had just received the biggest surprise of his career so far.

CHAPTER 15

SELECTED FOR THE ENGLAND SENIOR TEAM!

Jadon had just finished a tiring training session at Dortmund when he checked his phone and found a mind-blowing message waiting for him.

'Congratulations,' it read, 'you've been selected for the England squad.'

What?! After the Under-17 World Cup, Jadon had moved up to play for the Under-19s, but this message wasn't from one of the coaches there, or from the Under-21s either. No, it came from the senior England set-up. Following his super-sub performances for Dortmund, Jadon had been called up to the first team!

Wait a minute, was it one of his friends playing a prank on him? But no, when he checked, England confirmed it – his call-up was definitely not fake news! Jadon couldn't wait to tell his parents.

'That's amazing – I'm so proud of you!'

'Thanks, Mum, I couldn't have done it without you!'

'Well done, son. Don't forget to keep working hard, though.'

'Don't worry, Dad, I won't!'

On 4 October 2018, Gareth Southgate made his official England squad announcement for the UEFA Nations League matches against Croatia and Spain, and sure enough, there was Jadon's name, in between Marcus Rashford and Raheem, his old mentor at Manchester City:

'JADON SANCHO'

Wow, it was really happening! 'Proud day for me and my family,' he tweeted. 'Truly honoured and blessed.'

During the summer, Jadon had been a loyal England supporter, cheering on the seniors as they reached the semi-finals of the 2018 World Cup in Russia. It had inspired him to keep working hard, and now just three months later, here he was, part of the squad!

From the moment he arrived at St George's Park, Jadon set out to impress his manager and show that he was ready to shine. The training camp was a great chance for him to learn from superstars like Raheem and Harry Kane, but his main aim was to make his England debut.

In the first game against Croatia, Southgate started with his first-choice front three: Marcus, Harry and Raheem. With fifteen minutes to go, however, the score was still 0–0. What England needed was a gamechanger...

'Jadon, get warmed up – you're coming on!'

With a smile, he jumped off the subs bench and began doing his stretches along the touchline. Then, after listening to Southgate's instructions, Jadon took off his bib and his training top to reveal his white shirt, with Number 22 on the back. He was ready. This was it, the big moment he'd been waiting for. At the age of 18 years and 201 days, he was about to become the tenth youngest player ever to represent England!

Sadly, however, there were no loud cheers from

family and friends as Jadon ran onto the pitch, only a 'Good luck, bro!' from Raheem as he came off. Croatia weren't allowed to have any fans at their home games, and so the match was being played in an empty stadium. It was so quiet that you could hear every call, every kick and every tackle! It reminded Jadon of playing youth team football, but he was determined to enjoy his England debut, despite the strange atmosphere.

For the final fifteen minutes, Jadon ran and ran, up and down the right wing. He closed down the opposition defenders like he did at Dortmund, and he attacked at every opportunity. With stuttering steps, Jadon dribbled at the Croatia left-back, daring him to try and tackle him. One v one, his body swerved to the left, then the right, but in the end, his cross was blocked.

Moments later, Jadon tried again, only this time, everything was faster and more dangerous – the run, the stepovers, the body swerves. When a defender dived in, Jadon skipped past him and managed to deliver a cross, which flew just over Harry's head.

'Unlucky, son!' Southgate clapped and cheered on the sideline.

Jadon really didn't want his England debut to end, but before he could change the game, the final whistle blew. 0–0. Oh well, hopefully he would get another chance soon...

Jadon stayed on the bench for the second match against Spain, but a month later, Southgate selected him to start in a friendly against the USA at Wembley. Legend Wayne Rooney was making his 120th and final appearance for England, but it was the team's rising stars who stole the show...

Midway through the first half, Jadon got the ball on the right side of the box. Should he go for goal? Should he try one of his tricks? No, he had two defenders in front of him, so instead he made the wise decision to wait for Trent Alexander-Arnold to race forward from right-back. Jadon's pass was so perfect that Trent was able to shoot first time. *2–0!*

'Yessssssss!' The two England youngsters celebrated together, arm-in-arm, in front of 68,000 fans. It was a moment that neither of them would ever forget. Trent had his first international goal and Jadon had his first international assist. The future was theirs.

Three days later, England were losing 1–0 to Croatia with twenty minutes to go. Could Jadon come on and make an impact? Yes, he could! With his speed and skill, he helped push the team forward on attack after attack, until eventually the goals arrived.

Jesse Lingard grabbed the equaliser after a goalmouth scramble. *1–1!*

Then Harry slid in to score the winner. *2–1!*

What a comeback – England were through to the first-ever UEFA Nations League finals! The tournament would be taking place in Portugal in June 2019, and after a strong start to his senior international career, Jadon was really hoping he would get to play.

First, however, he had a Bundesliga title to win with Dortmund.

CHAPTER 16

DORTMUND'S DERBY HERO

8 December 2018, Arena AufSchalke, Germany

What a season Dortmund were having! After thirteen games, they were still unbeaten in the Bundesliga, and seven points clear at the top of the table. So, could they keep their great form going and become Champions of Germany for the first time in seven years? A 3–2 win over Bayern Munich had been a significant step towards Dortmund claiming the title, and now it was time for their next tough test – The Ruhr Derby against Schalke 04.

The '*Revierderby*' was famous for being one of the fiercest rivalries in German football. The two teams

weren't just battling for three points; they were battling
for local pride too. The previous two derbies had been
very disappointing for Dortmund: a 4–4 draw at home,
followed by a 2–0 loss away. Jadon had played the last
fifteen minutes of that dreadful defeat, and so this time
he was determined to lead his team to victory at the
Arena AufSchalke.

'Let's goooooooo!'

Jadon was growing in confidence with every game
he played. Since becoming a starter back in October, he
had:

Scored his first Bundesliga double against Hertha
Berlin,

Destroyed the Bayern defence with his dribbling,

Set up Dortmund's winner against Mainz,

And put on a spectacular skills show against
Freiburg.

With his team already winning 2–0, Jadon had
decided that it was time to have some fun. When
two Freiburg players surrounded him in his own half,
he spun away from both of them with an amazing
Maradona Turn.

Woah!

Then, as two more opponents surrounded him, he managed to escape again. How? By doing another Maradona Turn!

WOAH!

What a magician! And for his next trick, Jadon was going to win the derby, for his team and also for his nana, who had sadly died earlier that week. He had taken a few days off to be with his family, but now he was back and ready to be Dortmund's derby hero.

The atmosphere in the arena was electric, even before the match kicked off. Most of the stands were coloured Schalke blue, but there was one corner of Dortmund supporters dressed in yellow and black, who were making as much noise as they could.

When the referee blew his whistle, the battle on the pitch began. From the very first minute, the pace of the game was frantic, with tackles flying in everywhere, and action at both ends. In the seventh minute, Thomas flicked on Marco's free kick. *1–0 to Dortmund!*

What a start! Jadon tried and tried to create magic and make it 2–0, but in the end, the second goal of the game went to Schalke instead. The referee awarded a penalty for a foul by Marco and Daniel Caligiuri scored from the spot. *1–1!*

Game on!

As the second half went on, Jadon grew more and more frustrated. He was supposed to be Dortmund's gamechanger, but how could he shine when Schalke kept fouling him every time he got the ball?! Jadon didn't give up, though. He got back up and battled on, looking for a different way to win the derby for Dortmund. With twenty-five minutes to go, he swapped wings, moving from the right to the left. Maybe he'd have more luck on the other side of the pitch…

'Yes!' Jadon called for the ball and Manuel delivered it. Right, he was ready to go! With a stepover to the right and a body swerve to the left, he skilled his way past one Schalke player and then passed infield to Raphaël Guerreiro.

'One-two!' Jadon cried out as he carried on running into the penalty area. At top speed, he was unstoppable. When the pass arrived, he didn't rush his shot. Instead,

Jadon dribbled towards the six-yard box and then *BANG!* He calmly slid the ball past the Schalke keeper's outstretched arm and into the bottom corner. *2–1!*

Goooooooooooooooooooaaaaaaaaaaaaaaaaallllllllllllllllllllllllll!!!!!!!!!!!!!!!!!!!!!!

> *SAAAAAAANCHO!*
> *SAAAAAAANCHO!*
> *SAAAAAAANCHO!*

Thanks to him, Dortmund were winning the derby, but in that moment, Jadon was thinking of his nana. His wondergoal was for her, and for his baby brother who continued to inspire him. After kissing his hands, he pointed them towards the sky and then fell to the grass, overcome with emotion. Burying his face in his hands, he lay there for a while as his teammates came over to congratulate and comfort him.

'Respect, J – what a hero!'

'The fans will love you forever for that!'

'Yesssss – you did it, you legend!'

Their work wasn't done yet, though. They still had lots of defending to do, and so Jadon got back up and carried on fighting for his team. Five minutes later, he almost scored again, but in the end, the match finished 2–1. For the first time since 2015, Dortmund had won the Ruhr derby!

'Yesssssssssss!' roared the passionate supporters up in the stands, and so did the players down on the pitch. The victory meant so much to every single one of them, but for Jadon, their hero, it was extra special. Long after the final whistle, he stood with his teammates in a line, bouncing up and down together in front of the Dortmund fans. It was an experience that Jadon would remember for the rest of his life.

'Great feeling to get the winning goal in the big derby,' Jadon wrote on social media once the players finally left the pitch. 'Been a tough week personally, dedicating my goal to my Nana!'

CHAPTER 17

FRIENDS ON FIRE
IN THE BUNDESLIGA

'Woah JS, that goal was SICK!'

'Proud of you, bro – with everything you've been going through, that was some performance.'

'Yeah but wait until we play each other in a few weeks – my team's definitely gonna win!'

Jadon wasn't the only young Englishman enjoying life in the Bundesliga. In fact, there was a whole WhatsApp group of players who had moved to Germany in search of first-team football, including:

West Ham centre-back Reece Oxford, who was on loan at FC Augsburg in the south;

Jadon's old Manchester City academy teammate Rabbi Matondo, at Dortmund's rivals Schalke in the north;

Everton forward Ademola Lookman, who had been on loan at RB Leipzig in the east,

And most exciting of all, Jadon's best friend from South London, Reiss, who was on loan at 1899 Hoffenheim in the west.

The 'Brits Abroad' were so busy on the football pitch that they hardly ever saw each other, but they still sent each other lots of supportive messages throughout the season.

'Nice one, Reece!' Jadon wrote when his friend made his Augsburg debut against Mainz.

'Yesss, Rabbi!' Jadon wrote when his friend made his Schalke debut against Borussia Mönchengladbach.

Reiss, meanwhile, was flying high at Hoffenheim. In his first seven games for the club, he scored six goals.

'That's two more than you!' he joked with Jadon.

'Yeah, but I'm five ahead on assists, and I'm only just getting started!'

They were both delighted to see the other doing so well, but when would they get to play against each other in Germany? They couldn't wait for that day. As the Dortmund vs Hoffenheim game got closer, their friendly rivalry grew fiercer and fiercer.

'Watch out, bro – I've got my shooting boots on now!' Jadon warned after grabbing his sixth goal of the season against Borussia Mönchengladbach.

So, Jadon vs Reiss – who would be the winner? Reiss started on the bench for Hoffenheim, but he came on with twenty minutes to go. By then, however, Jadon had already put on one of his best Bundesliga performances yet.

When he picked up the ball on the left side of the pitch, the space was crowded, so Jadon cleverly passed back to Łukasz Piszczek and then raced over to the right for the one-two. When he got the ball back, Jadon burst into the box and from a difficult angle, he slid a perfect shot through the defender's legs, past the goalkeeper's outstretched arm, and into the far corner of the net. *1–0!*

Goooooooooooooooooooooaaaaaaaaaaaaaaaaalllllllllllllll lllllllllllll!!!!!!!!!!!!!!!!!!!!

'Come onnnnnnn!' Jadon roared as he jumped up

and punched the air. Another big game, another big game-changing goal. And as he'd warned Reiss before the match, Jadon was only just getting started. Ten minutes later, he set up Mario to make it 2–0, and in the second half, he backheeled the ball through a defender's legs to Mario, who set up Raphaël to score the third goal.

'Hurraaaaaaaaay!' they celebrated together in front of the cheering fans. What a touch from Jadon and what a magnificent team move!

With Bayern Munich back to their best and climbing up the table, Dortmund knew that they had to keep on winning in order to stay top of the Bundesliga. At 3–0 up, they seemed to be cruising to a comfortable victory, but when Reiss came on, he helped inspire a crazy Hoffenheim fightback.

Ishak Belfodil's shot crept over the goal line. *3–1!*

Pavel Kadeřábek headed in at the back post. *3–2!*

And with five minutes to go, Belfodil equalised with a diving header. *3–3!*

Nooooooo! On the edge of the Dortmund box, Jadon turned away in disbelief, his hands on his head and his mouth open wide. How on earth had they managed to throw the game away like that? A draw meant Bayern were now just five points behind them!

After the final whistle, though, Jadon put his frustrations aside and went over to have a chat and a hug with Reiss. 'Happy to get a goal and also to share the pitch with my close friend,' he tweeted later that night. 'It's been 1 hell of a journey bro but proud of you brother, keep working hard!'

So, could Dortmund hold on and lift the league title, or would Bayern catch them? Jadon did his very best to keep his team on top:

He scored a beautiful volley in a 3–2 win over Leverkusen, which was named the Bundesliga Goal of the Month;

He won an important penalty with his wonderful dribbling skills against Stuttgart;

He set up goals for Dan-Axel Zagadou and Marco to beat Hertha Berlin;

And then another for Paco in a win over Wolfsburg.

What a sensational first full season Jadon was having! He had the most assists in all of Europe's top five leagues and in March, he was named the Best Teenager in the World. Wow, what an amazing achievement! But while he was proud to win such a prestigious award, Jadon's main goal was to win the Bundesliga title with his team.

'Come onnnnn, we can do this!' the Dortmund players and supporters declared with confidence.

With seven games left, Dortmund were still two points clear at the top, but their next game was going to be the biggest and toughest of them all: Bayern Munich away. And with the pressure on, Dortmund collapsed to a devasting 5–0 defeat in the 'Der Klassiker'.

Oh dear, was that the end of their title hopes? No way, Dortmund were only one point behind Bayern with six games to go – anything could happen! While the thrashing had been a humiliating blow, Jadon refused to give up. They just had to keep winning and hope for the best.

A week later, Jadon scored both goals as his team beat Mainz 2–1. And to make the weekend even better, the next day, Reiss came off the bench to find the net for Hoffenheim too. The best friends were on fire in the Bundesliga!

But despite Jadon's twelve goals and eighteen assists, Dortmund's season ended in disappointment. On the final day, it was their rivals Bayern who lifted the league title, for the seventh time in a row.

Oh well, Dortmund would just have to win it next year instead. Jadon wasn't going to be a one-season wonder in Germany. No way, after becoming the Assist King of the Bundesliga and winning the Newcomer of the Year award, he was determined to come back even better – with more exciting skills, more dangerous dribbles, more goals, more assists, and more game-changing moments.

First, however, Jadon was off to Portugal to try to win a trophy for England...

CHAPTER 18

STEPPING FORWARD FOR ENGLAND PART I

Yes, Jadon's wish had come true – thanks to his magical performances for Dortmund, he had made the England squad for the UEFA Nations League finals!

After all the fun and success he'd had with the Under-17s in 2017, Jadon couldn't wait to experience his first senior international tournament. Okay, so England would only be playing two matches this time – a semi-final against the Netherlands and then, hopefully, the final – but still, there was a trophy up for grabs at the end of it!

Jadon was expecting Southgate to use him as a super sub, but no, the team news for the semi-final was even better than that. With Harry Kane still

recovering from an injury, Marcus Rashford moved
into the middle to play as a striker and Jadon took his
spot on the right wing.

What an opportunity! This was a huge chance for
him to step up and shine for his country like he had
all season for his club. Jadon had played very well
in his last game for England, setting up the first goal
for Raheem in a 5–0 win over the Czech Republic.
Beating the Netherlands, however, would be a much
bigger challenge. At the back, they had two of the best
defenders in the world: Virgil van Dijk and Matthijs de
Ligt.

Jadon, however, showed no fear. When he was at
his flying best on the football pitch, he was confident
that he could make a fool of any defender in a one
v one situation. In the first few minutes, he weaved
his way past the Dutch right-back, Denzel Dumfries,
with ease and delivered a cross that almost reached
Raheem. Then later on in the first half, de Ligt came
rushing towards him at speed, but with a roll of his
right foot, Jadon slid it straight through his legs.

MEGS!

What an entertaining wing wizard! By then, England were already winning, thanks to a penalty from Marcus. And early in the second half, Jadon got a glorious chance to make it 2–0. As Fabian Delph whipped a brilliant ball in from the left, he made a clever late run into the middle and found himself unmarked on the edge of the six-yard box. BOOM! Jadon got plenty of power on his header, but the ball flew straight at the Dutch keeper and safely into his arms.

'Nooooooo!' Jadon groaned with his hands on his head. What a bad, big-game miss – he really should have scored his first senior goal for England!

That turned out to be Jadon's last chance of the match. Five minutes later, Southgate subbed him off, and he had to watch from the bench as the Netherlands fought back to win the semi-final 3–1 in extra-time.

'If only I hadn't wasted my big opportunity!' Jadon muttered to himself as he slumped lower in his seat.

Onto the next game! Instead of competing in the UEFA Nations League final against Portugal, England

were taking on Switzerland in the Third Place Play-off, but it was still a match they really wanted to win. With captain Harry back, Jadon dropped down to the bench, but he came on to make an important contribution for his country. Because after another 120 minutes of goalless football, the game went to…
PENALTIES!

Uh-oh – Harry Kane had already gone off and Marcus was injured, so who would England's five takers be?

1) Harry Maguire… SCORED!

2) Ross Barkley… SCORED!

3) Jadon! Yes, even at the young age of nineteen, he had the courage and the confidence to step forward for England at this crucial moment. 'If you believe, you can achieve' – that's what he always told himself. As he walked from the halfway line to the penalty area, however, the pressure was really on because so far, all four spot-kicks had been successful. Was he going to become a national hero or villain?

When the referee blew the whistle, Jadon skipped two paces to the left and then jogged up to the spot.

With the side of his right foot, he guided the ball carefully and accurately into the corner of the net. *GOAL!*

Pressure, what pressure? Phew, he was a national hero now! As the fans clapped and cheered, Jadon walked calmly back to join his teammates for the rest of the shoot-out…

4) Raheem… SCORED!

5) Jordan Pickford… SCORED!

With ten penalties taken, neither team had missed a single one, so it was time for sudden death. Eric Dier scored for England, which meant that Josip Drmic had to do the same for Switzerland. He stepped up and struck the ball powerfully… but Jordan threw himself athletically across the goal to make a super save!

Yesssssss, England were the winners! No, they hadn't lifted the Nations League trophy, but it was always nice to win a penalty shoot-out, especially after so many painful losses in the past. The national team was making progress – from finishing fourth at the World Cup in 2018, to third in the Nations League in 2019, to who knows… The Euros final in 2020? That was Southgate's exciting plan for England, and Jadon was desperate to be a part of it.

A few months later, he was selected to start alongside Harry and Raheem in the front three for their second Euro qualifier against Kosovo. It was another incredible opportunity to impress his manager, and Jadon was determined to make the most of it this time.

With half-time approaching and England winning 3–0, Raheem dribbled up the left on another attack. Just before he entered the box, he thought about shooting himself but instead he kindly passed the ball across to his young friend on the opposite wing. This was it – the moment Jadon had been waiting for, the moment he had been dreaming about since he was a young kid...

Jadon refused to rush it, though. He calmly took one touch to steady himself,

A second to shift the ball a little to the right,

And then with his third touch, he fired a low shot past the Kosovo keeper.

Goooooooooooooooooooooaaaaaaaaaaaaaaaaalllllllllllllll

/////////////////!!!!!!!!!!!!!!!!!!!!!!!

Jadon kissed the three lions on his England shirt and then threw his head back and roared with a mixture of joy and relief. He had his first senior international goal at last, and his second followed just two minutes later. Jadon was now an unstoppable superstar, for club and country.

CHAPTER 19

BEATING
BAYERN!

3 August 2019, Westfalenstadion, Germany

Back at Dortmund, Jadon couldn't wait for the
new season to start and what a game to begin – the
German Super Cup against their bitter rivals, Bayern
Munich.

'It's time for revenge,' Jadon told Marco as the
players prepared for the big match. Beating Bayern
would be a perfect way to kick off the new campaign.
'They won the league, but WE are winning this
trophy!'

Jadon was feeling full of confidence after scoring
a hat-trick in a friendly against FC Zürich a few days

earlier. Sure, Bayern had much better defenders like David Alaba and Jérôme Boateng, plus Manuel Neuer in goal, but Jadon believed that he could beat anyone! So far in his three appearances against the German champions, he had zero goals and zero assists.

'But that's all about to change,' Jadon assured himself as the two teams waited in the tunnel.

Over the summer, Dortmund had signed two exciting new wingers, Thorgan Hazard and Julian Brandt. Jadon was pleased to see the squad improving, but now he needed to prove himself as the club's number one option on the right.

'Let's goooooooo!'

Dortmund had home advantage for the Super Cup, and what an advantage it was. As Jadon and his teammates walked out onto the pitch, there was the amazing Yellow Wall of supporters all around them, creating an extra-special atmosphere.

Their energy and passion really inspired the players, who came out fighting from the very first minute. They pressed brilliantly in defence and looked dangerous in attack. Dortmund were the team on top, and Jadon was at the centre of everything:

Chipping a beautiful pass through to Paco, who shot just wide,

Then flicking a clever ball on to Marco, who dribbled at the defence.

At half-time, however, the score was still 0–0. Had Dortmund wasted their best chance to beat Bayern?

No! Just after the break, Jadon intercepted a pass from Thiago Alcântara near the halfway line, turned and raced forward at speed. Boateng came out to close him down, but with a last-second body swerve, Jadon skipped straight past him. On the edge of the box, he was surrounded by four Bayern players, but somehow he managed to escape and poke a pass through Corentin Tolisso's legs to Paco in the middle. *BANG!*... *GOAL – 1–0!*

Yessssss, Dortmund were winning the Super Cup! As the players celebrated, the Yellow Wall around them went wild.

The trophy wasn't quite theirs yet, though. To beat a brilliant team like Bayern, Dortmund were going to need to stay focused right until the final whistle. From the opposition, Robert Lewandowski nearly headed in an equaliser, then Leon Goretzka fired over the bar, then Marwin Hitz made a super save to stop Kingsley Coman, and Manuel cleared a Thomas Müller shot off the line.

Dortmund were under constant pressure in defence; could they really hold on for another thirty minutes? No, what they really needed to do was score the second goal themselves…

Raphaël won the ball back on the edge of his own box, and looked up for someone to pass to. A-ha – he spotted Jadon in lots of space, racing up the right wing, ready to launch a lightning counter-attack. Perfect – *PING!*

ZOOM! Alphonso Davies chased back as fast as he could, but even he couldn't catch Jadon. He was away, past the halfway line and towards the penalty area.

SANCHOOOOOOOOO!
SANCHOOOOOOOOO!
SANCHOOOOOOOOO!

Usually, Jadon liked to try out tricks as he dribbled,

but not this time. Instead of skill, he used his speed to make a direct sprint into the box. Marco and Paco were both waiting in the middle, but Jadon decided to go for goal himself. Why not, especially after his hat-trick against FC Zürich? He took his time to steady himself and then with a swing of his right leg, he shot low and hard… through Neuer's legs – *2–0!*

Goooooooooooooooooooaaaaaaaaaaaaaaaaallllllllllllll llllllllllll!!!!!!!!!!!!!!!!!!!!

What a sensational, solo strike! It was Jadon's second game-changing moment of the match, and it was even greater than the first. Cupping his ear to the crowd, he ran towards the corner flag and then leapt up and punched the air with passion. 'Come onnnnnnnnnnnnnn!' he roared up at the Yellow Wall.

Game over? After twenty more minutes of determined defending, the final whistle blew and Dortmund were the 2019 German Super Cup winners! Just like Jadon had hoped, they'd got their revenge and the trophy too.

'We did it!' Jadon yelled, as he ran around the pitch with a huge smile on his face. He had hugs for each and every teammate: Marco, Paco, Raphaël, Manuel… Not only had they just beaten Bayern, but Jadon had also won the first senior trophy of his professional football career! Oh and the man of the match award too. It had to be him, Dortmund's hero. With his skill and speed, Jadon had been the star of the show, setting up the first goal and scoring the second.

With flip-flops on his feet and a winner's medal around his neck, Jadon joined his teammates on the stage in the centre of the pitch to wait for the best moment of all – the trophy presentation. As their captain Marco collected the glistening silver Super Cup, the anticipation began to build around the stadium.

Ohhhhhhhhhhhhhhhhhhhhhhhhhhhh…

Until eventually, Marco lifted the trophy high above his head.

'…Hurrrraaaaaaaaaaaaaaayyyyy!' Jadon cheered, throwing his arms up as yellow and black confetti filled the air.

What a start to the new season! But could

Dortmund keep their good form going in the Bundesliga? On the opening day, they went 1–0 down to Augsburg in the very first minute, but back they came to win in confident style. And who was their hero at the centre of everything once again?

Jadon slipped the ball through to Marco, who crossed it to Paco. *1–1!*

Jadon fired in at the back post. *2–1!*

When the Augsburg keeper failed to deal with Jadon's dangerous cross, Marco pounced on the rebound. *3–1!*

Jadon weaved his way into the box and then passed to Paco. *4–1!*

'New season, same Sancho,' some said on social media. But the truth was, Jadon was looking even better than before.

CHAPTER 20

RISING TO THE CHAMPIONS LEAGUE CHALLENGE

While Jadon loved winning in the Bundesliga, what he was looking forward to most was the return of his favourite football tournament, the greatest club competition in the world... the UEFA Champions League!

Ever since his early days at the Watford academy, it had been Jadon's dream to play for one of Europe's top clubs and compete in the Champions League. It was the highest level in the game, the competition that separated the stars from the superstars, and Jadon was determined to become a superstar.

Jadon had high hopes for 2019–20, his second season in the Champions League. His first season had been a fun but also frustrating experience, from the high of scoring his first goal against Atlético Madrid in the group stage, to the low of losing to Harry and Dele Alli's Tottenham in the Last 16.

Jadon had improved a lot since then, though. Now, he was older, wiser, and a more consistent gamechanger. He would need to be because Dortmund were in the 'Group of Death', along with Slavia Prague, Inter Milan and Barcelona. Wow! Only the top two teams would go through to the knockout stage, but Jadon was excited by the challenge, not scared.

'Let's gooooo!' he tweeted. This was his chance to test himself against world-class defenders like Stefan de Vrij, Gerard Piqué and Jordi Alba, and world-class attackers like Romelu Lukaku, Antoine Griezmann, and best of all, Lionel Messi!

First up for Dortmund was a home game against the mighty Barcelona. Jadon took a little while to get into the game, but when he did, he made a difference yet again. From wide on the wing, he dribbled at the left-back, teasing him with his trademark body swerves.

Nélson Semedo thought he'd done a good job of stopping Jadon, but just before the ball went out of play, the winger cut back with a Cruyff Turn and the defender caught him on the foot.

'Arghhhhhhhhh!' Jadon cried out in pain.

Penalty! Up stepped Marco, but sadly his spot-kick was saved by Marc-André ter Stegen. Noooooooo! After that, Dortmund tried and tried, but the ball just wouldn't go in. How were they not winning? Despite all their chances, the match ended 0–0.

'Well played,' said Messi, shaking Jadon's hand at the final whistle.

Never mind, a draw wasn't a bad result against a team like Barcelona; Dortmund would just have to do better in their next matches. However, after winning 2–0 away at Slavia Prague, they lost 2–0 away at Inter Milan. Uh-oh, were they crashing out of the competition already?

Dortmund absolutely had to win their next home game against Inter Milan, but at half-time, they found themselves 2–0 down. Although their Champions League chances really didn't look good, Jadon and his teammates refused to give up. Early in the second half, Achraf Hakimi pulled one goal back, and then Julian equalised. Game on! There was still time for Dortmund to find a winner…

In the seventy-seventh minute, Achraf dribbled his way up the right wing and then passed inside to Jadon. He had four Inter players around him, but luckily, he knew exactly what his teammate would do: keep running into the box for the one-two. Jadon's pass was inch-perfect, delivering the ball between two defenders and into Achraf's path for him to strike first time past the keeper. *3–2!*

Dortmund's incredible comeback was complete and the Westfalenstadion was rocking! Jadon had experienced some very special nights in front of the Yellow Wall, but that was certainly one of the most memorable.

With two games to go in the Group of Death, Dortmund were up to second place, but their next match was the most difficult of all – Barcelona away. Could they shock the Spanish giants? No, at the Nou Camp, Messi was at his magical best, grabbing a goal and two beautiful assists. Woah! Jadon could only watch and admire, and then attempt to create some magic of his own. After controlling a pass from Julian, he spun, shifted the ball quickly to the right, and then unleashed an unstoppable shot into the top corner. *3–1!*

Goooooooooooooooooooooaaaaaaaaaaaaaaaaaalllllllllllllll llllllllllll!!!!!!!!!!!!!!!!!!!!

Woah! It was a wonderstrike, worthy of Messi himself. It deserved a proper celebration, but his team were losing, so Jadon just jogged back to the halfway line.

That defeat meant that Dortmund would now need to beat Slavia Prague at home to go through to the next round. That sounded possible, but Jadon made sure of it with another big game performance.

In the tenth minute, Julian played it through to Marco, who passed across to Jadon. *1–0!*

Slavia Prague equalised just before half-time, but Jadon had one more trick up his sleeve. From the left side of the box, he slipped a no-look pass through to Julian, who scored at the near post. *2–1!*

'Yessssssss!' Jadon cheered as he celebrated with his teammates.

With that win, plus Barcelona beating Inter, Dortmund had done it; they had escaped from the Group of Death!

'Last 16!' Jadon posted with pride.

The games didn't get any easier for Dortmund, though. This was the Champions League, the greatest club competition in the world. So, after the challenge of Messi, Griezmann and Suárez, now in the next round, they faced PSG's fantasy front four: Neymar Jr, Kylian Mbappé, Edinson Cavani and Ángel Di María.

Woah! Dortmund, however, had superstar attackers of their own: Jadon, Marco, and in January 2020, they were joined by Erling Haaland. The young Norwegian striker had signed for £18 million, after scoring twenty-eight goals in only twenty-two games for Austrian club Red Bull Salzburg.

Erling and Jadon – it looked like a match made in heaven. They were two teenagers with incredible football talent, and their different strengths made them a highly dangerous duo. Erling was tall, powerful and a fantastic finisher, whereas Jadon was smaller, with more speed and skill. What a dream team!

In the German Bundesliga they had got off to a great start together. With Dortmund losing 3–1 at Augsburg, Erling came on to make his debut in the fifty-sixth minute. Three minutes later, he scored his first goal, after a beautiful through-ball from Jadon, and two minutes after that, Jadon got the second and equalised. By the final whistle, Erling had a hat-trick and Dortmund had won 5–3! In total, they scored ten goals between them in their first three games. But the big question was: could they shine against a top team like PSG?

In the home leg at the Westfalenstadion, Erling changed the game with two superb, second-half goals: a quick-reaction rebound, followed by a ferocious shot from the edge of the box. *2–1 to Dortmund!*

'What a strike!' Jadon yelled as he joined the pile of Dortmund players on top of Erling. Woah, this new guy was really, really good!

After the final whistle, Jadon hugged Neymar Jr and

then swapped shirts with Mbappé, but Dortmund's job wasn't done yet. No, there was a still a second leg to play in Paris...

At the Parc des Princes, both teams had chances to score, but while PSG took theirs, Dortmund didn't.

Jadon volleyed wide, then Neymar Jr headed in. *1–0!*

Julian's shot deflected just over the bar, but Juan Bernat's flick landed in the bottom corner. *2–0!*

And with that, Dortmund's Champions League campaign came to a disappointing end. While it was frustrating to lose in the Last 16 again, their young superstars were still learning about playing at the highest level. Jadon could tell that there were exciting times ahead, especially with Erling.

CHAPTER 21

EXCITING TIMES WITH ERLING

The 2019–20 season felt like the same old story for
Jadon at Dortmund – crashing out in the Champions
League Last 16 and then coming second behind Bayern
Munich in the Bundesliga. Runners-up again! His own
stats, however, were getting better and better. As well
as equalling his record of eighteen assists, Jadon also
finished with seventeen league goals, five more than the
previous season, which made him Borussia Dortmund's
top scorer!

He was proud of every single strike:

His left-foot finish against FC Köln,

His opening goal against Hertha Berlin,

His equaliser against RB Leipzig,

His winner against Freiburg,

His calm shot into the bottom corner against Frankfurt,

And Jadon's favourite memory of all: his first professional hat-trick against Paderborn!

As he prepared for the 2020–21 season, Jadon was looking forward to lots more amazing moments like that, and hopefully, he could help Dortmund to win another trophy, especially now that he had Erling alongside him in attack.

Thanks to lots of hard work in training, they knew each other's game even better now – where they wanted the ball, what runs they would make and when. Now that they had developed that deeper understanding, Dortmund's duo were looking more dangerous during every match they played together.

In their first Bundesliga game, Jadon carried the ball all the way from his own box to the Bayer Leverkusen box at the other end. When he got there, two defenders closed him down, so Jadon coolly slipped the ball through for Erling, who chipped the keeper. 3–0!

'Mate, you're the best!' Erling shouted, shaking Jadon

with excitement as they celebrated together.

A few weeks later in the big Ruhr Derby against
Schalke, they teamed up again. As he dribbled forward,
Jadon poked a beautiful pass into Erling's path and he
lifted the ball over the keeper. *2–0!*

Together, they made scoring goals look so easy
and entertaining, and they even had a fun new goal
celebration to share. After pointing at each other,
they pointed to their own heads to show their special
connection, before finishing with kung-fu kicks.

'Yesssssss!' Jadon cheered as he jumped happily into
Erling's arms.

That win kept Dortmund level on points with Bayern
in second place, but soon afterwards, Erling suffered
a hamstring injury, and then the bad results began to
build up: a 2–1 loss against FC Köln, a 1–1 draw with
Frankfurt, then a 5–1 thrashing by Stuttgart! After
that embarrassing defeat, Lucien Favre was sacked as
manager and replaced by Edin Terzić for the rest of the
season.

Oh dear. To turn things around, Dortmund desperately
needed to have their two biggest stars back to their best.

Thankfully, at last, in early 2021, Erling and Jadon were both fit and on form again. Hurray! Away at top four rivals RB Leipzig, Jadon scored Dortmund's first goal and then delivered a brilliant curling cross for Erling to head in the second. Yes, that was more like it – the dream team was back together! Jadon and Erling celebrated with hugs, jokes and big high-fives.

By February, however, Dortmund were still way down in sixth place. Their chances of winning the Bundesliga title were long gone, but they were desperate to finish in the top four. If they didn't, there would be no Champions League football next year! No – Jadon and Erling couldn't let that happen without a fight. That was the least they could for the club's incredible fans.

'Come on, we've got some catching up to do!'

That would begin with the second Ruhr Derby of the season. Jadon loved playing away at the Arena AufSchalke, and he gave Dortmund the lead with a curling shot into the top corner. Then two minutes later, he chipped a lovely ball into the box for Erling, who finished with an incredible flying volley. Woah, what a stunning goal from Dortmund's superstar duo!

Just as they were leading their team back up the table together, however, it was Jadon's turn to suffer a muscle injury. The timing was terrible. Not only would he have to miss six Bundesliga games, but he would also miss his team's big Champions League quarter-final clash with his old club, Manchester City. Nooooooo! Without him in the squad, Dortmund lost both legs of the quarter-final and again crashed out of the competition.

Jadon returned to the team just in time for its last four games of the Bundesliga season. Dortmund were still fifth, four points behind Frankfurt, but the fight still wasn't over…

Erling got the winning goals against Wolfsburg,

And Jadon got the winning goals against RB Leipzig.

Jadon set up two goals to beat Mainz,

And Erling scored two goals to beat Bayer Leverkusen.

In the end, Dortmund finished above Wolfsburg as well as Frankfurt, in third place. Hurray, job done – thanks to their superstar duo, they had qualified for the Champions League! What would Dortmund do without them? And that wasn't all; Jadon and Erling had also led Dortmund to the final of the DFB-Pokal, Germany's big cup competition.

Jadon had been the star of the tournament so far, grabbing four goals and four assists in only five games. So, could he carry that form into the cup final against RB Leipzig and help Dortmund lift the trophy?

In only the fifth minute, Jadon got the ball on the left and dribbled into the box. He could see Erling making a run in the middle, but as the Leipzig defenders backed away, Jadon decided to go for goal himself. Why not? With a whip of his right foot, he curled a beautiful shot past the diving keeper and into the far corner of the net. *1–0!*

Goooooooooooooooooooooaaaaaaaaaaaaaaaaaallllllllllllllllll lllllllll!!!!!!!!!!!!!!!!!!!!

'Let's goooooo!' Jadon cried out, slapping his chest, the air, and even the corner flag! It was one of his best goals for Dortmund, and definitely the most important. In their biggest game of the season, he had stepped up like a superstar to give them the lead.

'What a start!' Erling shouted as he sprinted over to celebrate with his friend.

After that, there was only one winning team. Marco

set up Erling and then Jadon to make it 3–0 before half-time. And late in the second half, Jadon sprinted forward on another counter-attack and passed to Erling, who added a fourth goal.

So Dortmund were the 2021 German Cup Winners! And with two goals each, Jadon and Erling were the heroes. It was a wonderful feeling that words couldn't describe. After the trophy celebrations, they walked around the pitch together, posing for photos and taking it in turns to hold the huge gold cup.

'Nah, I don't want to let go yet!' Jadon said with a cheeky smile as Erling tried to grab the trophy off him.

At the end of a difficult, up-and-down season, it was time for the Dortmund players, coaches and supporters to celebrate and enjoy their success. After all, who knew what next year would bring, and whether or not their superstar duo would still be there at the club...

CHAPTER 22

STEPPING FORWARD FOR ENGLAND PART II: EURO 2020

Was Dortmund's Assist King on his way back to the Premier League? The transfer rumours were already flying, but all that could wait. For now, Jadon was fully focused on his next football challenge: Euro 2020, delayed by a year to summer 2021 because of the global COVID-19 pandemic!

On 1 June 2021, Gareth Southgate announced his final England squad for the tournament, and in amongst the eight attackers, there was his name:

'JADON SANCHO'

Yessssss, he had made it! It was a dream come true to be representing his country at a major tournament. Since the 2010 World Cup, Jadon had watched them all on TV, but this time, he would be an England player, rather than a supporter.

'Euro 2020 let's go!' he posted proudly on Instagram with a photo of him in the new national team shirt.

At twenty-one, Jadon was one of the youngest members of the England squad, but that didn't matter because everyone got on really well with each other at St George's Park, no matter how old they were or what club team they played for. For the next few weeks, they were all on the same team, working together to win the same trophy.

But what would England's starting line-up be? There was so much competition for places all over the pitch, and especially in attack. There was only really one spot up for grabs in Southgate's first-choice front-three. It would be Harry, Raheem – and who else???

Raheem preferred to play on the left side of the attack, so it was a right winger that England needed. Perfect, that was Jadon's favourite position, but sadly he wasn't the only one in the squad who could play there. The manager had so many excellent options to choose from, each with a different style and with different strengths:

Jadon,

His old City friend Phil,

Marcus,

Bukayo Saka,

And Jack Grealish.

So, what could Jadon do to stand out above the rest? Southgate picked him to start in England's second pre-tournament friendly against Romania, but he struggled to find that killer final pass and his best shot hit the crossbar. In their 1–0 win, it was Jack who won the penalty, and Marcus who scored it. Arggghhh – had Jadon wasted his big opportunity to impress?

In England's opening game of Euro 2020 against Croatia, it was Phil who started on the right, with Marcus coming on after seventy minutes. And Jadon? Sadly, he didn't even make the matchday squad. Never mind, the England win was the most important thing, and they had got it, thanks to Raheem's second-half goal.

The next day in training, Jadon continued to concentrate on working hard and 'Woah!'-ing the coaches with his skills. He was enjoying his Euro 2020 experience, but he was desperate to play his part on the pitch for England. Oh well, there were still two more group games to go…

But Jadon, disappointingly, would stay on the subs bench during the 0–0 draw against Scotland, and he only played the last ten minutes against the Czech Republic. While it was great to get some game-time, by then, they had already won. Would that be it, Jadon's one and only appearance for England at Euro 2020? No – Southgate was just waiting for the right kind of game, where his young winger would be able to attack with freedom, as he loved to do.

That 'right kind of game', though, wasn't the Round of 16 clash with old rivals Germany. No, for that match, the England manager picked Bukayo for his energy and his defensive qualities, and brought on Jack to change the game in the last twenty minutes.

But how about the quarter-final against Ukraine? Fortunately for Jadon, for that match, the England

manager moved Jadon into the starting line-up.
Hurray, at last! It was one of Jadon's happiest and
proudest moments as he walked out onto the pitch at
the Stadio Olimpico in Rome and stood alongside his
teammates to sing the national anthem.

'Let's gooooo!' Jadon cheered as he high-fived
Raheem before kick-off. It was time to shine. What
could he do to change the game and keep his place in
the team?

From wide on the right wing, Jadon raced infield
with the ball, playing a one-two with Kalvin Phillips,
then another with Mason Mount, before passing to
Raheem on the left. Woah!

Later on, as he collected the ball in his own
half, Jadon could see two opponents closing in. No
problem! With two quick taps, he danced past the first
and then with a late body swerve, he weaved past the
second. *Woah!*

Yes, Jadon showed flashes of his skill on the right
and caused lots of problems for the Ukraine defenders,
but unfortunately, most of the main action came down
the left for England.

Raheem passed through to Harry Kane, who poked the ball past the keeper. *1–0!*

Luke Shaw curled in a free kick and Harry Maguire scored. *2–0!*

Luke crossed to Harry Kane. *3–0!*

England were on fire! Jordan Henderson scored a fourth, and Jadon dribbled forward looking for a fifth, but a defender tackled him just as he entered the box. Nearly! Still, at the final whistle, it was hugs and high-fives all round. Job done – they were through to the Euro semi-finals!

'Big performance from the team tonight!' Jadon tweeted. 'Always an honour to represent my country.'

Despite that promising performance, however, Jadon dropped back down to the bench for the semi-final against Denmark. Bukayo started on the right wing, and when England went searching for a winner in extra-time, Southgate sent on Phil and Jack instead. Although Jadon was disappointed, he didn't show it; they were all on the same team, working together to win the same trophy. In the 102nd minute of the match, Raheem was fouled in the penalty area.

Harry Kane's spot-kick was saved, but he scored the rebound. 2–1!

When the final whistle blew, Jadon raced onto the pitch with the rest of the subs to congratulate his teammates. Yessssss, England were on their way to the Euros final for the first time ever! What an achievement! The celebrations went on long after the final whistle at Wembley, both on the pitch and in the stands. With a big smile on his face and an arm around Raheem's shoulder, Jadon joined in with the full squad singalong in front of the fans:

...It's coming home, it's coming home,
It's coming, FOOTBALL'S COMING HOME!'

...SWEET CAROLINE!
Da-da-da,
Good times never seemed so good,
So good, so good, so good!

The England team had already made history, but could they go all the way and lift the trophy? In the final against Italy, Jadon started on the bench again and it looked like he might stay there when Luke scored in only the second minute. 1–0 to England! What a start! In the second half, however, Leonardo Bonucci equalised and the game was still tied late in extra-time. They were seconds away from a penalty shoot-out, so the England manager made two last substitutions:

Jordan Henderson off, Marcus on,

Kyle Walker off, Jadon on!

It was a risky tactic when they hadn't even touched the ball, but Southgate wanted to have his five best penalty takers on the pitch:

1) Harry Kane... SCORED!

2) Harry Maguire... SCORED!

3) Marcus... HIT THE POST!

Noooooo!

4) Jadon! He had to score – the pressure was really on now. With a look of calm determination on his face, he walked forward from the halfway line and placed the ball down on the spot. Come on, he could do this! After a deep breath, he took one big step back and then three stuttering steps forward. *BANG!* Jadon

aimed for the same corner as he had in the Nations League shoot-out against Switzerland, but the Italy keeper Gianluigi Donnarumma dived the right way and he was big enough to reach it... SAVED!

Noooooo!

Jadon turned away in despair, throwing his hands to his head and then down over his face. In the biggest moment of his career, he had missed. He had failed, and it was the worst feeling in the world.

The final wasn't over yet, though. Jordan Pickford made a super save to keep out Jorginho's penalty, which meant that England could equalise if they scored their last spot-kick...

5) Bukayo... HAD HIS SHOT SAVED TOO!

NOOOOO!

Now it really was over – England had lost, and Italy were the Euro 2020 winners. On the halfway line, Jadon couldn't hold the tears back any longer. He felt like he had really let his team and his country down.

'No, you haven't,' Southgate told Jadon as he sobbed into his shirt. 'Not at all. Remember, we win together, we lose together. It was my decision for you to take that penalty and you were brave enough to step forward when I asked you to. So, be proud of yourself and don't worry, we'll be back!'

Jadon took a few days to reflect on his Euro 2020 final experience, but eventually he felt ready to speak out, not only about the penalty miss but also about the horrible racist abuse he, Marcus and Bukayo had received on social media afterwards:

'Hate will never win. To all the young people who have received similar abuse, hold your heads up high and keep chasing your dream. I am proud of this England team and how we have united the whole nation in what has been a difficult 18 months for so many people... It's been an honour as always representing England and wearing the Three Lions shirt, and I have no doubt we'll be back even stronger!'

CHAPTER 23

MOVING TO MANCHESTER UNITED

Jadon was too much of a positive person to spend the rest of the summer feeling sorry for himself. Plus, he didn't have time for that. In July 2021, just two weeks after the Euro 2020 final, he was back in the news and this time for a much happier reason: he was moving to Manchester United!

'THE WAIT IS FINALLY OVER,' Jadon tweeted with a photo of him wearing the famous red shirt. After more than a year of rumours and rejected offers, the deal was finally done. For £73 million, Jadon was on his way to Old Trafford, and Dortmund's dream team was splitting up.

'Good luck on your next journey bro, we had some

good times together!' Erling posted on Instagram.
'Can't wait to see you shine!'

Jadon was really going to miss his friend and
everyone else at the club. 'I just want to start off by
thanking Borussia Dortmund for everything they
have done for me,' he wrote in an emotional goodbye
message, 'taking the risk on a young 17 year old at the
time with no first team experience and believing in
me.'

After four seasons, two trophies, 137 appearances,
fifty goals and sixty-six assists, it felt like the right
time for Jadon to leave Germany and return home
to England to prove himself in the Premier League
at last. He was joining one of the most exciting
young strikeforces in the world: while he was on the
right, Marcus Rashford was on the left, and Mason
Greenwood in the middle, with Bruno Fernandes
and Paul Pogba creating chances in midfield. Wow
– maybe Manchester United were finally ready to
challenge for the top trophies again!

It certainly seemed that way as The Reds started the
season with a 5–1 win over Leeds United and Jadon

played his first fifteen minutes in the Premier League. And by 31 August, United's title chances looked even better as they announced another amazing signing – Cristiano Ronaldo was coming home!

It was massive news for the club, but what did it mean for Jadon? He had only just arrived in a big-money deal, and already he was being overshadowed. Jadon was going to need time to adapt to the speed and style of the Premier League before he hit top form, but United now had seven senior forwards fighting for just three starting spots:

Cristiano,

Marcus,

Jadon,

Mason,

Edinson Cavani,

Anthony Martial,

And Jesse Lingard.

There was so much attacking talent in one squad, there was no time for patience. No, Jadon was under pressure to perform straight away. When he played poorly against Newcastle, the manager Ole Gunnar

Solskjær subbed him off after sixty minutes and dropped him to the bench for the next three games.

Oh dear – Jadon's Manchester United dream was quickly turning into a nightmare. After his rapid rise for Dortmund and England, he was used to shining straight away, but so far, his Premier League record stood at seven games, zero goals and zero assists. Not good enough at all.

'Sancho – what a waste of money he was!' supporters were already starting to say.

Jadon wasn't the only one struggling at Manchester United, though – the defence was making lots of mistakes and the whole team looked so disorganised and sluggish. Something was going seriously wrong at the club, but no-one seemed to know how to fix it. First, they lost to Aston Villa, then Leicester City, and after that, the defeats got even more embarrassing:

5–0 to big rivals Liverpool,

2–0 to City in the Manchester derby,

And, worst of all, 4–1 to Jadon's old team, Watford!

A massive club like Manchester United couldn't carry on losing like that; when they slipped down to seventh place, Solskjær was sacked. While they searched for a new manager, Michael Carrick took charge for their crucial Champions League game against Villarreal, and who did he choose for his front three?

Cristiano,

Anthony,

And Jadon!

Hurray – this was the fresh start Jadon needed, a new chance to prove himself at Manchester United. Although he had lost some confidence, he hadn't lost any of his determination. And so he played with his old energy and passion, defending with discipline and then attacking at every opportunity, especially in the second half...

Jadon cut inside off the right wing and played a one-two with Bruno. When the ball came back to him, he dribbled past the last defender and went for goal, but the keeper made a good save. Unlucky, but that was much more like the Jadon that Dortmund fans knew and loved!

Seven minutes later, Manchester United took the

lead thanks to a clever lob from Cristiano, and there was still time for the team to score an even greater goal. On the counter-attack, Cristiano passed the ball through to Marcus, who played it across to Bruno, who flicked it on to… Jadon! This was the golden chance that he'd been waiting for all game long, and he wasn't going to waste it. He took a calm touch to control the ball and then fired a swerving shot into the top corner. *2–0!*

Gooooooooooooooooooooaaaaaaaaaaaaaaaaaallllllllllllll llllllllllll!!!!!!!!!!!!!!!!!!!!

'Yesssssss, come onnnnnnn!' Jadon cried, leaping up to punch the air and let out all of his frustration. At last, he was off the mark at Manchester United! Finally, he had his first goal for his new club, and hopefully, the first of many.

From South London, to Manchester, to Germany, and then back to Manchester – again and again, young Jadon had shown the courage and the confidence to take on new challenges, as well as the talent to become one of the biggest superstars in the world.

Borussia Dortmund

🏆 DFL Supercup: 2019

🏆 DFB-Pokal: 2020–21

England Under-17s

🏆 FIFA U-17 World Cup: 2017

Individual

🏆 UEFA European Under-17 Championship
Golden Player: 2017

🏆 VDV Newcomer of the Season: 2018–19

- 🏆 Bundesliga Team of the Season: 2018–19, Goal.com NxGn Best Teenager in the World: 2019
- 🏆 DFB-Pokal top goalscorer: 2020–21

SANCHO

25 **THE FACTS**

NAME: Jadon Malik Sancho

DATE OF BIRTH: 25 March 2000

PLACE OF BIRTH: Camberwell, London

NATIONALITY: English

BEST FRIEND: Reiss Nelson

CURRENT CLUB: Manchester United

POSITION: RW

THE STATS

Height (cm):	180
Club appearances:	199
Club goals:	76
Club assists:	78
Club trophies:	2
International appearances:	23
International goals:	3
International trophies:	1
Ballon d'Ors:	0

★ ★ ★ **HERO RATING: 85** ★ ★ ★

GREATEST MOMENTS

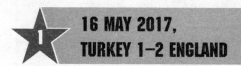

16 MAY 2017,
TURKEY 1–2 ENGLAND

Jadon was on fire throughout the UEFA European Under-17 Championship, grabbing five goals and five assists, as well as the Golden Player Award. He scored a stunning strike against Ireland in the quarter-finals, and in this semi-final against Turkey, he produced two match-winning moments. First, Jadon set up Callum Hudson-Odoi and then he scored a goal of his own. What a future superstar!

8 DECEMBER 2018, SCHALKE 1–2 BORUSSIA DORTMUND

After a promising start in Germany, Jadon's form absolutely exploded in his first full season there. There were lots of game-changing moments, but this one in the Ruhr Derby against Schalke was one of the best. Just days after the death of his nana, Jadon showed the strength and skill to score a brilliant winner and become the Dortmund hero.

3 AUGUST 2019, BORUSSIA DORTMUND 2–0 BAYERN MUNICH

After finishing second behind Bayern in the Bundesliga, Dortmund got revenge against their rivals in the German Super Cup. Jadon was the man of the match, setting up the first goal with a magical run and pass to Paco Alcácer, and then scoring the second himself on the counter-attack. After sprinting forward from his own half, he finished by nutmegging Manuel Neuer. Hurray – Jadon had his first senior trophy!

10 SEPTEMBER 2019, ENGLAND 5–3 KOSOVO

This Euro 2020 qualifier was only Jadon's fourth senior start for England, but he took his chances like an experienced striker. As half-time approached, his strike partners Harry Kane and Raheem Sterling had both already scored, so they helped set up Jadon for his first two international goals. England's new wing wizard was off the mark!

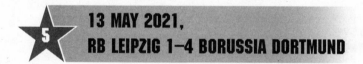

13 MAY 2021, RB LEIPZIG 1–4 BORUSSIA DORTMUND

Dortmund won this DFB-Pokal cup final in style, thanks to two goals each from their dream team, Jadon and Erling Haaland. Jadon's first was especially good, a curling shot into the far corner of the net in only the fifth minute of the match. What a matchwinner! For Jadon, it was his first-ever major trophy, and for Dortmund, their first in four years.

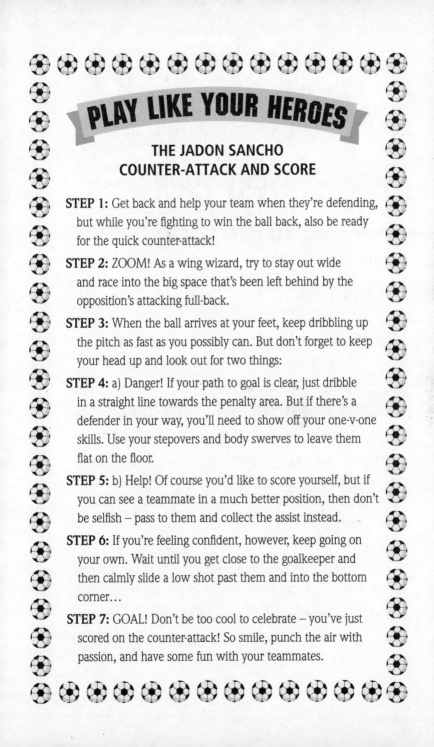

PLAY LIKE YOUR HEROES

THE JADON SANCHO
COUNTER-ATTACK AND SCORE

STEP 1: Get back and help your team when they're defending, but while you're fighting to win the ball back, also be ready for the quick counter-attack!

STEP 2: ZOOM! As a wing wizard, try to stay out wide and race into the big space that's been left behind by the opposition's attacking full-back.

STEP 3: When the ball arrives at your feet, keep dribbling up the pitch as fast as you possibly can. But don't forget to keep your head up and look out for two things:

STEP 4: a) Danger! If your path to goal is clear, just dribble in a straight line towards the penalty area. But if there's a defender in your way, you'll need to show off your one-v-one skills. Use your stepovers and body swerves to leave them flat on the floor.

STEP 5: b) Help! Of course you'd like to score yourself, but if you can see a teammate in a much better position, then don't be selfish – pass to them and collect the assist instead.

STEP 6: If you're feeling confident, however, keep going on your own. Wait until you get close to the goalkeeper and then calmly slide a low shot past them and into the bottom corner...

STEP 7: GOAL! Don't be too cool to celebrate – you've just scored on the counter-attack! So smile, punch the air with passion, and have some fun with your teammates.

TEST YOUR KNOWLEDGE

QUESTIONS

1. What did Jadon and his friends on the estate call the place where they played football together?

2. At the age of seven, Jadon joined Watford instead of which other Premier League club?

3. Jadon and Reiss Nelson won the football tournament at the 2011 London Youth Games playing for which team/borough?

4. Growing up, who was Jadon's favourite football hero?

5. True or false – Jadon won the FA Youth Cup with Manchester City.

6. In 2017, Jadon was regarded as one of Manchester City's three most promising young players – but who were the other two?

7. Which nation did Jadon's England Under-17s lose to in the Euros final, but then beat in the World Cup final a few months later?

8. The Borussia Dortmund fans are famous for creating an amazing atmosphere, but what is their nickname?

9. Who set up Jadon's first two goals for England against Kosovo in 2019?

10. Jadon scored two goals for Dortmund in the 2021 DFB-Pokal cup final. Who scored the other two?

11. Who was the Manchester United manager when Jadon scored his first goal for his new club?

1. *Blue Park.* **2.** *Arsenal.* **3.** *Southwark.* **4.** *Ronaldinho.*
5. *False – his team lost to Chelsea in the final in 2016 and 2017.*
6. *Brahim Díaz and Phil Foden.* **7.** *Spain.* **8.** *The Yellow Wall.*
9. *Raheem Sterling.* **10.** *Erling Haaland.* **11.** *Michael Carrick.*